Maryport. A Roman Fort and its Community

MARYPORT

A ROMAN FORT AND ITS COMMUNITY

DAVID J. BREEZE

ARCHAEOPRESS

Archaeopress Publishing Ltd
Summertown Pavilion
18-24 Middle Way
Oxford OX2 7LG

www.archaeopress.com

ISBN 978 1 78491 801 9
ISBN 978 1 78491 802 6 (e-Pdf)

© Archaeopress and David J. Breeze 2018

Cover illustrations:
In the background: Maryport looking north with the whaleback ridge on which the fort sits beyond the town, the Solway Estuary beyond and Criffel. to the left. This was published, uncoloured, in J. C. Bruce, *The Roman Wall*, 3rd edition, London: Longmans etc, 1867, opposite p. 366

Back cover: The boar, the symbol of the Twentieth Legion, and now the logo of the Senhouse Museum Trust

On the back flap: The logo of the Senhouse Museum Trust

All rights reserved. No part of this book may be reproduced, or transmitted, in any form or by any means, electronic, mechanical, photocopying or otherwise, without the prior written permission of the copyright owners.

This book is available direct from Archaeopress or from our website www.archaeopress.com

For Joe Scott Plummer
Custodian of the Netherhall Collection

Contents

List of Figures iii

Preface 1

Ancient and Modern 4

The Roman army at Maryport 17

The extra-mural community 43

Religion at Maryport 55

Maryport in its setting 84

Life on the edge of empire 92

Final thoughts 102

Acknowledgements 107

Further Reading 108

Index 114

List of Figures

An aerial view of the fort at Maryport vi
Figure 1.   The coat of arms of Humphrey Senhouse I dating to 1726 4
Figure 2.   William Camden, author of *Britannia* 5
Figure 3.   The altar drawn by Sir Robert Cotton in 1599, now in the British Museum 6
Figure 4.   Camden noted this inscription at Netherhall in 1599 7
Figure 5.   The Senhouse family, its excavations and visitors to Netherhall 8
Figure 6.   The drawing of the north gate 9
Figure 7.   The section cut through Pudding Pie Hill 10
Figure 8.   Netherhall in the 19th century 13
Figure 9.   Some of the altars and sculpture displayed in the portico 13
Figure 10. Netherhall and the River Ellen in the 19th century 14
Figure 11. The Naval Reserve Training Battery 14
Figure 12. A corner in the museum where some of the altars are displayed 15
Figure 13. A view of Maryport from the south in the second half of the 19th century 18
Figure 14. The signpost marks the distance to Rome 19
Figure 15. A view of the hill on which sits the Roman fort 19
Figure 16. An aerial view of the fort at Maryport looking south-east 20
Figure 17. The visible remains of the north gate 21
Figure 18. The sculpture of a gate 22
Figure 19. F. A. Child's drawing of the west gate at Housesteads 22
Figure 20. A drawing of part of the commanding officer's bath-house 23
Figure 21. A putative lay-out for the fort 24
Figure 22. A building inscription of the Emperor Hadrian found at the fort at Moresby 25
Figure 23. The excavation of what is believed to be the intervallum street of an early fort 26
Figure 24. The ditch of the Roman camp below the temple looking south 27
Figure 25. A building inscription recording work at Maryport 27
Figure 26. A simple record of the Twentieth Legion working at the fort 28
Figure 27. The boar, emblem of the Twentieth Legion 28
Figure 28. An altar of L. Cammius Maximus 29
Figure 29. Peter Connolly's painting of a cavalryman and infantryman 30
Figure 30. An altar dedicated by M. Maenius Agrippa 31
Figure 31. An altar dedicated by C. Caballius Priscus 32
Figure 32. The altar to Jupiter dedicated by Helstrius Novellus 32
Figure 33. The altar dedicated by C. Cornelius Peregrinus 33
Figure 34. This unusual stone was dedicated by P. Postumius Acilianus 33
Figure 35.   An altar dedicated by T. Attius Tutor (*RIB* 838) 34

Figure 36. A map of the Roman empire 37
Figure 37. L. Antistius Lupus Verianus stated that his city of origin was Sicca in North Africa .. 38
Figure 38. The altar dedicated to Jupiter by L. Cammius Maximus 38
Figure 39. This altar erected by M. Censorius Cornelianus 39
Figure 40. The tombstone of Julius Marinus 40
Figure 41. The tombstone of a man from Galatia, which can be read in the 3rd line 41
Figure 42. A dedication in Greek to Asclepius by A. Egnatius Pastor 42
Figure 43. This tile bears the inscription, COH I HISPA|INDVTIVSFEC 42
Figure 44. The tombstone of Julia Martina 45
Figure 45. A female figure wearing an ungirt Gallic tunic and cloak around the shoulders 46
Figure 46. A female figure wearing a foot-length girt Roman tunic and palla 47
Figure 47. A fragment of a glass bangle found at Maryport 47
Figure 48. The geophysical survey 49
Figure 49. Joseph Robinson's plan of his discoveries 51
Figure 50. The house excavated by Joseph Robinson 52
Figure 51. The house excavated by Oxford Archaeology North looking north-west 53
Figure 52. Chain mail dating to the 2nd or 3rd century 54
Figure 53. J. Collingwood Bruce at the entrance to the keep of Newcastle castle 56
Figure 54. J. C. Bruce's plan of the altar pits 56
Figure 55. The altar pits as revealed by the excavations of Ian Haynes and Tony Wilmott 56
Figure 56. This altar by C. Caballius Priscus records the name of the regiment he commanded .. 57
Figure 57. This altar, also dedicated by C. Caballius Priscus, states only his name with the name of his regiment 57
Figure 58. A sacrificial scene on the Bridgeness distance slab on the Antonine Wall 59
Figure 59. Maenius Agrippa dedicated this altar to Jupiter and the Deity of the Emperor 59
Figure 60. The altars found in the shrine at Osterburken 61
Figure 61. The plan of the temple and circular building 62
Figure 62. The temple following excavation by Ian Haynes and Tony Wilmott 63
Figure 63. The plan of the temple excavated by Ian Haynes and Tony Wilmott 64
Figure 64. The plaque recording a dedication to *Iupiter Optimus Maximus Capitolinus* 65
Figure 65. This is probably the head of a deity 66
Figure 66. A dedication to Military Mars by T. Attius Tutor 66
Figure 67. A dedication to Neptune 67
Figure 68. A dedication to Volcanus/Vulcan by Helstrius Novellus 67
Figure 69. A statue of Vulcan, possibly unfinished 67
Figure 70. Hercules on the side of an altar 68
Figure 71. The goddess Minerva holding a spear and shield 68
Figure 72. A sculptural depiction of a gate with a lady, presumed to be Venus 68
Figure 73. This damaged head may represent Mercury 69
Figure 74. A dedication to Eternal Rome and Fortune the Home-Bringer 69
Figure 75. T. Attius Tutor dedicated this altar to the Emperor's Victory 70
Figure 76. The Victory of the Emperors 70
Figure 77. The dedication to the Valour of the Emperor by Hermione 71
Figure 78. A triad of possible Sea Nymphs 71
Figure 79. A woodcut showing the triad before part of the stone was lost 71
Figure 80. A goddess sitting on a chair holding a possible cornucopia 72
Figure 81. The statuette of a Genius – the god or spirit of the place 73
Figure 82. The god Sol on the keystone of an arch 73
Figure 83. A horned god holding a spear and a rectangular shield 74
Figure 84. The depiction of a Celtic god 74
Figure 85. The phallus of Marcus Septimius 74

Figure 86. A phallic stone 74
Figure 87. A phallic stone 74
Figure 88. The goddess Epona... 75
Figure 89. A Chi-Rho symbol on a stone now lost... 76
Figure 90. The fir cone 77
Figure 91. Two burials in the cemetery... 78
Figure 92. The stone recording Rianorix... 79
Figure 93. The cemetery north of the 1870 altar find spot 79
Figure 94. The Serpent Stone as it is today.. 80
Figure 95. The Serpent Stone as found... 80
Figure 96. The face on the Serpent Stone 81
Figure 97. One of the heads found at Burrow Heights near Lancaster............................. 81
Figure 98. The tombstone of a cavalryman... 82
Figure 99. The damaged tombstone which probably depicts a soldier 83
Figure 100. The cliffs of Maryport today looking towards the museum 84
Figure 101. The pattern of military deployment in northern England.............................. 85
Figure 102. The probable line of the Roman road to the east of Maryport 86
Figure 103. The plan of the rural settlement excavated 88
Figure 104. Composite aerial view of the rural settlement 89
Figure 105. A section across the ditch of the rural settlement excavated 89
Figure 106. Plan of the settlement at Ewanrigg 90
Figure 107. Swarthy Hill as viewed from the fort at Maryport.. 90
Figure 108. An artist's impression of the Roman fortlet at Barburgh Mill in south-west Scotland. 93
Figure 109. Criffel as viewed from the fort at Maryport 94
Figure 110. A coin of the Emperor Hadrian 95
Figure 111. The milefortlet at Swarthy Hill 97
Figure 112. A reconstructed gate of the late Roman fort at Cardiff................................... 98
Figure 113. The south-west corner of the fort 99
Figure 114. The tombstone of [S]purcio 99
Figure 115. The excavation of a house in the extra-mural settlement............................ 103
Figure 116. A recently discovered altar, dedicated by T. Attius Tutor 103
Figure 117. An artist's impression of the interior of a Roman fort 104
Figure 118. Two belt stiffeners... 105
Figure 119. An altar to the goddess Setlocenia dedicated by Labareus........................... 106

An aerial view of the fort at Maryport looking south-east; the museum lies to the bottom right on the top of the cliff. Photograph Nick May

Preface

In 1599, towards the end of the reign of Elizabeth I, William Camden and Sir Robert Cotton came to a place called Ellenborough, later renamed Maryport after Mary Senhouse, in Cumberland, now Cumbria. The reason for their visit was to view some Roman altars. Camden was the author of a book called *Britannia*, a compilation of archaeological and historical – and curious – information about the British Isles. He had written about Ellenborough in the second edition of his book, published in 1587, and now he was here to see the place for himself, and meet its owner, John Senhouse. The date is important for it indicates that the Senhouse family had already started creating the collection which is now housed in the Senhouse Roman Museum in Maryport. The mention of John Senhouse is equally important because he is the first named custodian of the collection, which is now in the ownership of his 10th great-grandson, Joe Scott Plummer, who, in 1990, placed his ancestral inheritance, the Netherhall Collection, into the care of the Senhouse Museum Trust.

Since the visit of William Camden and Robert Cotton, successive generations of Senhouses have added to the collection, generally through investigating Roman buildings in the fort and the extra-mural settlement to its north. Occasionally plans were made; rarely were the discoveries located on a map. As a result, the precise origin of most of the inscriptions and items of sculpture discussed below cannot be located. Sometimes we are lucky. The chance disturbance of a stone by a ploughman in 1870 led to the finding of no less than 17 Roman altars in a series of pits. A decade later, a meteor flashed across the fields of Roman Maryport when Joseph Robinson, manager of the local branch of the Cumberland Union Banking Company, spent many days in the Spring and Summer of 1880 excavating the area north of the fort, and publishing a report. However, this local bank manager soon got into financial difficulties and was dismissed from his post, moving to London. Fortunately, the baton was picked up by J. B Bailey, a local schoolmaster, who, for nearly 50 years from 1880, faithfully recorded further work and catalogued the collection.

It was only in 1966 that the first modern excavation took place at the site. This was followed in the current century by investigations south-west of the fort by the Maryport and District Archaeological Society, within the extramural settlement by Oxford Archaeology North and in the religious quarter by Professor Ian Haynes and Tony Wilmott of Newcastle University on behalf of the Senhouse Museum Trust, while further work took place in a small cemetery and an adjacent Roman farmstead to the south of the fort directed by CFA Archaeology based in Edinburgh.

In 1964, Lieutenant Commander Brian Ashmore, another Maryport hero, brought the collection together in the stables of Netherhall and in 1985 he established the Senhouse Museum Trust which now has the care of the altars, sculpture and other items in the Netherhall collection housed in the museum in the Naval Battery on Sea Brows on the northern edge of Maryport. Here it is displayed thanks to a long-term loan by Joe Scott Plummer.

The aim of this book is to bring together information about the site and the collection and to offer an account of the Romans at Maryport, the officers and their soldiers, the civilians, in life and in death, in short, an account of life on the north-west frontier of the Roman Empire.

The corners of the fort face the cardinal points of the compass; traditionally, however, the north-east rampart of the fort has been termed the north side, and this convention will be retained. As most of the measurements were given in imperial units, I have retained these, providing the metric equivalent in brackets. I have not provided references within the text. A list of publications relating to Maryport and the wider issues discussed below is at the end of the book. The illustrations are all copyright Senhouse Museum Trust unless otherwise stated. All dates are AD/CE except where stipulated.

Edinburgh
16 January 2018

A note on names

Maryport has a confusing nomenclature. In the meander of the River Ellen beside its mouth is a mound, Castle Hill. This is a small medieval ringwork castle with a rampart and ditch, probably dating to the 12th century. Its defensive purpose was renewed in the 20th century when a gun was placed on its summit. The castle lay within the manor of Alneburgh, held from the time of Edward I (1272-1307) by the Eaglesfields. In the 14th century they moved to a more comfortable location on the flat ground beside the river a little upstream. Here, using the conveniently located Roman stones, they built a pele, a tower house, which they named Alneburgh. This is the medieval spelling of Ellenborough. In 1773 the Rev. Erasmus Head still referred to it as Ellenborough-hall, though adding 'now called Nether-hall'. The hall lay north of the river in the parish of Crosscanonby, in whose church the Senhouses were buried.

South of the river lay the village of Ellenborough with the port at the mouth of the river named Ellenfoot or Elnefoot in records dating to 1688 and 1758. Today, the names Ellenborough and Ellenfoot survive in that part of Maryport lying to the east of the railway station.

In 1748 Humphrey Senhouse II started to develop a planned town north of the river between Castle Hill and the Roman fort and called it Maryport after his wife Mary Senhouse (née Fleming). Fleming Square commemorates her, and Curzon Street acknowledges the marriage between Blanche Pocklington Senhouse and Alfred Curzon, Baron Scarsdale; their son was George Curzon, Viceroy of India from 1899 to 1905, and the author of a treatise on frontiers. In 1894 local government reorganisation joined Ellenborough with Maryport and in 1929 Netherhall was transferred from Crosscanonby to Maryport.

Chapter 1

Ancient and Modern

I. Sinhous, a very honest man   William Camden

Early investigations

The Senhouse family were a local family, originally from Seascale, to the south of Whitehaven. The earliest record of the family was in the reign of Richard I – or his brother King John – that is, about 1200, when Walter de Sewynhouse was granted land in Cumberland. In 1529 his descendant John Senhouse married Elizabeth, daughter and co-heiress of Gawen and Mabel Eaglesfield (or Egglesfield) of Alneburgh Hall, later renamed Netherhall. The Roman fort which we call Maryport lay on their land. The elder son of John and Elizabeth retained the ancestral lands at Seascale, where his descendants were to remain for several centuries, while John, the younger son, inherited Alneburgh, and started, or perhaps continued, the collection of Roman altars (Figure 1).

Figure 1. The coat of arms of Humphrey Senhouse I dating to 1726. The arms of the Senhouse family are a parrot (this was actually a wooden popinjay painted like a parrot and used for target practice by archers) and they are quartered with those of the Eaglesfield family which were three eagles (top left). The other arms are those of families to which the Senhouses were related.

Figure 2. William Camden, author of *Britannia*

We know that the collection was in existence by 1587 because two altars were mentioned by William Camden in the second edition of his topographical account of the kingdoms of Britain, *Britannia* (Figure 2). William Stukeley stated that 'the Senhouses, and the Eaglesfields, whose heiresses they married, have been continually digging here' so it would appear that the history of the collection is even older. Camden and his friend and fellow antiquarian Sir Robert Cotton came north in 1599 and visited John Senhouse, 'a very honest man'. At the

Figure 3. The altar drawn by Sir Robert Cotton in 1599, now in the British Museum. This is the woodcut prepared for publication in J. C. Bruce, *Lapidarium Septentrionale*, 874; see Figure 33

Figure 4. Camden noted this inscription at Netherhall in 1599 and published this drawing in his *Britannia* (*RIB* 844); see Figure 76

time of their visit, 'the ancient vaults stand open, and many altars, stones with inscriptions, and Statues are here gotten out of the ground ... [and are] placed orderly about his house'. Cotton drew at least two of the inscriptions, including for *Britannia* (Figures 3 and 4); one was the altar which Stukeley later recorded had been found in the north-east corner of the fort on the *vallum*, that is, the rampart, and which is now on display in the British Museum. The travellers departed grateful for the 'right courteous and friendly entertainment' of John Senhouse.

John's descendants were to welcome many visitors to their house over the following centuries for their growing collection attracted scholars interested in Roman Britain (Figure 5). Alexander (Sandy) Gordon came from Scotland in 1725 and William Stukeley from Boston in Lincolnshire in the same year. Thomas Pennant came from Wales in 1772, and John Collingwood Bruce, the author of *The Roman Wall*, from Newcastle in 1870 and 1880.

The visitors described the state of the visible remains of the fort. Stukeley stated that it was 400 feet square with two ditches and three entrances – Gordon said four – with ruins of a 'city' to the north. Here can be traced the square plots of houses, paved streets worn with use, while the field walls were composed of Roman stones, some showing mouldings and other sculptures. Stukeley also usefully notes that the Eaglesfields were digging there before the Senhouses and 'hundreds of cart-loads of hewn stone' have been carried off. Gordon helpfully stated that the ramparts of the fort stood about 16 and 18 feet (4.9 and 5.5m) high, though he was prone to exaggeration.

Successive generations of Senhouses investigated the fort. The strong-room in the headquarters building was opened in or about 1686. An unfortunate

Senhouse family	excavation	visitors
John Senhouse (died 1604)		William Camden and Sir Robert Cotton, 1599
John Senhouse (died 1667)		William Dugdale, 1665
John Senhouse (1660-94)	vault in headquarters building excavated about 1686	
Humphrey Senhouse I (1669-1738)		William Stukeley, 1725 Alexander Gordon, 1725
Humphrey Senhouse II (1706-70)	Pudding Pie Hill, 1742 the civil settlement about 1742 and 1766	
Humphrey Senhouse III (1732-1814)	north gate, 1787 bath-house 1788	Thomas Pennant, 1787
Humphrey Pocklington-Senhouse (1843-1903)	altar pits 1870 Robinson excavated in the civil settlement 1880	J. C. Bruce, 1870

Figure 5. The Senhouse family, its excavations and visitors to Netherhall

precedent was set on this occasion for its floor slabs were removed. Humphrey Senhouse II re-opened the strong room in 1766, and recorded its measurements as 12 by 10 ft 6 in (3.66 by 3.20m) with the walls standing 3 ft 6 in (1.07m), and the steps much worn. His son, Humphrey III, investigated the site on at least five occasions from 1772 to 1788, and passed information to Hayman Rooke for publication in the journal *Archaeologia*; this is one of the earliest excavation reports to have been published in Britain. The areas examined included the north gate, where the arch was complete, and a bath-house (Figure 6). One building, recorded by Pennant in 1772, was plastered and painted 'with what is now pink color [sic]'. Unfortunately, much Roman stone was recycled to build the new town of Maryport, including the arch of the north gate. Another arch appears to have been re-used in Crosscanonby church.

It must be admitted that not all Senhouses were assiduous custodians of the collection. Several stones, such as the altar to the god Belatucadrus, which was lost sometime after 1599, and one of the Jupiter altars by the First Cohort of Spaniards, last seen in 1665 (though a fragment survives), have disappeared. The 17th century, unfortunately, saw the vogue of giving antiquities to friends. The large altar to the Genius of the place, recorded by Camden and Cotton in 1599, was given to Sir James Lowther in 1683 – it is now in the British Museum.

Figure 6. The drawing of the north gate published in *Archaeologia* 10 (1792) opposite p. 140

Less fortunate was the fate of one of Cammius Maximus's altars. Sometime between its discovery in 1704 and 1725 it was given to William Kirkby of Ashlack in Furness, father of Eleanor, the wife of Humphrey Senhouse I; it is now lost. Another went to the bishop of the Isle of Man. Nor was such giving restricted to those times. In 1935 Guy Senhouse sent one of the Jupiter altars as a present to Mussolini; that is now on display in the Museum of Roman Civilisation in Rome.

The connection between John Collingwood Bruce, later the doyen of Hadrian's Wall studies, and Maryport began in very different circumstances from the later archaeological link. Bruce undertook studies at Glasgow and Edinburgh Universities with the intention of becoming a Presbyterian Minister. In 1829 he was licensed as a preacher and undertook a peripatetic existence for the next few years travelling round the towns and villages of northern England. In September 1830, he was at Maryport and considering taking up a position there. He left the town in November and returned to Newcastle via Skinburness and Bowness-on-Solway where he inspected the remains of Hadrian's Wall. In December he returned to Maryport, staying into the following year, but in September 1831 he decided to abandon the ministry and join his father as a teacher in his school, the Percy Street Academy. Here, his love of history led him to the study of Hadrian's Wall, and back to Maryport.

In the first edition of *The Roman Wall,* published in 1851, Bruce recorded that the east gate was visible with its sill rutted to a gauge of 5 ft 10 in (1.78m), which he stated was very wide, and a well, presumably in the courtyard of the headquarters building. A later commentator noted some traces of masonry at the east gate which 'render it probable that this entrance was guarded by additional outworks', or perhaps that the gate towers projected beyond the fort wall. Bruce came to Maryport in 1870 to report on the discovery of a cache of 17

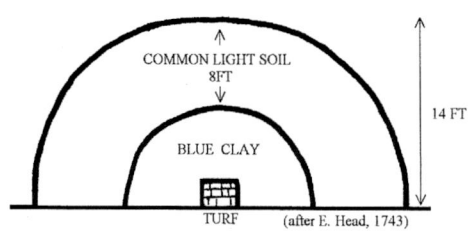

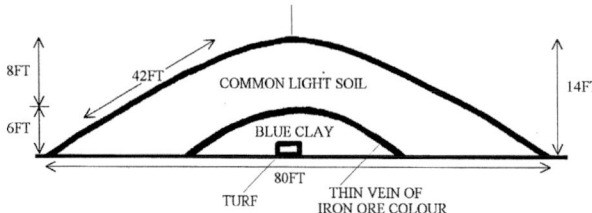

Figure 7. The section cut through Pudding Pie Hill, drawn by Shirley Waldock, the upper drawing showing the interior construction (after Head 1763), with the lower the projected outline extrapolated from Head's measurements

altars buried in pits to the north-east of the fort. He also usefully published a list of the coins preserved at Netherhall, which ended with the Emperor Honorius who reigned about 400.

It was not just the fort which received the attention of the Senhouses. To the south-west of the fort lay a mound known as 'The King's Burying Place', or more prosaically Pudding Pie Hill. In 1742 it was excavated by Humphrey II. We are fortunate to have a contemporary account. This records that the circumference of the mound was 'no less than 250 feet' (76m), and 14 ft (4.27m) high, partially damaged by ploughing (Figure 7). At the centre of the mound were three or four courses of turves many laid grass to grass. This was covered by blue clay about 6 ft (1.8m) thick over which was 'common light soil' about 8 ft (2.4m) thick; the two layers were separated by 'thin vein of the colour of iron ore', probably iron-pan. Beneath the turf were found the pole and shank bones of an ox (Pennant said, 'the bones of a heifer and of a colt') and wood ash. The description of the mound and the discoveries within it suggest that its purpose was funerary, and prehistoric rather than Roman.

One hundred and fifty years after the excavation, in 1891 to be exact, Pudding Pie Hill was interpreted as the saluting base beside a Roman parade ground by Father J. I. Cummins. Not a native of Maryport, his sojourn in the town was relatively brief and this was his only known foray into archaeology. His suggestion was based on his identification of an area beside the mound that he believed had been artificially levelled. This area was a parallelogram measuring about 95 by 93 yards (87 by 85 m). Earlier Ordnance Survey mappers had not recorded the 'parade ground' and modern scholarship has dismissed this interpretation. The erection of houses over the site in 1921 and 1922 destroyed both the level ground and the mound, which was finally removed in April 1922. Observations during construction work led to the location of the road leading out of the south gate and the recording of a course of cobbles set in clay 18 ft (5.5m) long to the south-west of the mound, but this was not dated.

The 1880s were notable years at Maryport. J. B. Bailey, a local school master, published a paper on the site in 1880, following it with a catalogue of the collection in 1915. A local bank manager, Joseph Robinson, recorded the finds discovered during the quarrying of stone for the new dock and, also in 1880, trenched north of the fort in order to plan the road system. Robinson's discoveries were numerous and included the temple and its adjacent circular structure, a strip building close to the north gate of the fort, the Serpent Stone and other altars and inscriptions, paving, burials, pottery and coins. Robinson's report provides a flavour of the investigations of the time. During the afternoon of 1 May 1880, the round building was first observed, and the line of its circular wall was then uncovered in an hour.

Further afield and shortly after the destruction of Pudding Pie Hill, discoveries on both sides of the mouth of the River Ellen were interpreted as being Roman in date. The 'foundations of a massive wall' were found south of the river and appeared to continue north to run to the west of the medieval motte. A second wall lay at right-angles south of the river. These walls enclosed a 'pavement'. J. B. Bailey, who recorded these remains, assumed them to be Roman, quoting Camden's mention of ruins at the mouth of the river. Neither the walls nor the pavement are dated; the former could relate to the medieval castle, while the latter is now regarded as a natural feature.

To the north, in Crosscanonby churchyard, two walls were found, 2 ft 6 in (760mm) wide, 30 ft (9m) apart, bonded in hard red mortar and placed on clay and cobble foundations. A large altar was also found there in 1877 during the digging of a grave.

The Roman fort at Maryport was chosen as the site of an excavation to mark the one hundredth anniversary of the Cumberland and Westmorland Antiquarian and Archaeological Society in 1966. The work was directed by Tony Birley and Mike Jarrett. Unfortunately, it was dogged by bad luck in that it coincided with an outbreak of foot and mouth disease and heavy rain which impeded progress, while the area chosen to investigate had suffered from severe stone robbing. 'The excavation consisted of a section through the eastern defences of the fort ... with the investigation of structures to the north of this line', where four different phases of buildings were uncovered spanning the occupation of the fort.

The collection

We have seen that in 1599 the Roman stones were placed around the house, which became known later as Netherhall. Stukeley recorded that 'the walls of the house are incrusted over, as we may say, with inscriptions, carvings and bas reliefs, taken from the ruins of the Roman city'. He also recorded a 'most stately altar placed in the middle of the garden, with a sun-dial on the discus. Some are somewhat more securely set up within the porch'. Stukeley also lamented that some stones were outside and exposed to the weather.

Later, it would appear that many items were displayed in a canopied portico or long loggia in Netherhall, and also a summer house in the garden which had been a small railway station (Figures 8 and 9). The last of the Senhouses to live at Netherhall was Guy Pocklington Senhouse. His household of 4 indoor servants was sadly reduced from the 20 servants and 2 gardeners recorded there at the beginning of the 20th century. When he died in 1952, his younger brother Roger inherited the estate but preferred to live in London where he was co-owner of the publisher Secker and Warburg. The house was vacated in 1962 and gradually deteriorated, exacerbated by a fire in 1979. Thereafter, the house was demolished until all that remains is the medieval tower-house (Figure 10).

When I first saw the collection in the late 1960s it was in the (leaking) stables where Brian Ashmore had brought the collection in 1964. Together with Mike Jarrett, he scoured the abandoned gardens of Netherhall in the search for missing stones and in spite of their efforts they were not able to find some objects such as the Chi-Rho inscription. Encouraged by their actions, local people handed in stones which they had previously acquired. It was not until a decade later that the bronze artefacts were re-discovered. Considering the long history of investigations at the site, these are few in number and yield relatively little information – the horse trappings, for example, offer no information on the status of the cavalry which we know were stationed at the site.

It was through the energy and connections of Brian Ashmore that a permanent home was found for the collection in the Battery on Sea Brows on the northern edge of Maryport. As a retired naval officer, Brian had connections with the Maryport Sea Cadets and when they vacated the building he stepped in. Erected

Figure 8. Netherhall in the 19th century; the long portico is presumably where most of the collection was displayed. Reproduced by kind permission of Tyne and Wear Archives and Museums

Figure 9. Some of the altars and sculpture displayed in the portico

Figure 10. Netherhall and the River Ellen in the 19th century.
Reproduced by kind permission of Tyne and Wear Archives and Museums

Figure 11. The Naval Reserve Training Battery, now the museum,
with a replica Roman tower to the right

in 1885 as a Naval Reserve Training Battery on land provided by the Senhouse family, transferred in 1908 to the Army (Volunteers), the building is of red sandstone with white dressings from the Admiralty's Portland quarries (Figure 11). The semi-circular tower in the centre, facing landward, is provided with mock machicolations. Guns were placed in the wings. The Battery was last used in 1980. Unfortunately, it was then badly damaged by vandals and had to be repaired. The Senhouse Museum Trust opened the Battery as a museum on 7 April 1990.

The Senhouse Museum Trust

The Trust was established in 1985 as a result of the perseverance of Brian Ashmore; its first chair was Professor Michael Jarrett. The task of those early years was to create a viable museum (Figure 12). Once established, the trust

Figure 12. A corner in the museum where some of the altars are displayed

considered a potential wider role. A research strategy was created. This stipulated that the first aim should be the publication of the collection (still not completed), then the recording of all physical remains through non-invasive techniques – in effect, geophysical survey – which has been achieved, and, finally, if excavation was considered it should be focused on improving understanding of the collection so that it can be better interpreted for members of the visiting public.

Accordingly, in 2010 the trust invited tenders for an excavation at the place where the 17 altars had been found in 1870 in the hope of better understanding the nature of their burial. The tender was won by Professor Ian Haynes of Newcastle University, with Tony Wilmott as the site director. The excavation was undertaken in 2011 and produced entirely unexpected results. Instead of being buried with care in keeping with their religious significance, the altars had been unceremoniously used as packing stones for timber uprights, presumably forming a building of some kind. As a result of this discovery, four further seasons of excavations were undertaken, to explore the pits further and the area to the south where the altars may have stood. This area contained the temple and circular building discovered in 1880. The excavations also provided evidence that the examination of the pits in 1870 was not the first antiquarian investigation of that part of the site, the earlier work having taken place before 1725, on the basis of the discovery of a fragment from an altar recorded at that date.

The Senhouse Museum Trust is not the only player in the Roman field of Maryport. Oxford Archaeology North undertook the excavation of a house in the civil settlement. CFA Archaeology Ltd, based in Edinburgh, excavated part of a cemetery and a rural farmstead south of the fort in advance of a housing development. Finally, the Maryport and District Archaeological Society investigated the children's playground to the south-west of the fort in 2002 and 2005. All these excavations will be discussed further in this book.

Chapter 2

The Roman army at Maryport

It hath a goodly prospect farre into the Irish sea. William Camden

The Roman fort at Maryport is in a superb location, looking over the Solway Estuary, with views to the south-west as far as the Isle of Man (Figures 13 and 14). It sits on the seaward side of a whaleback ridge, one of several along the Cumbrian coast. Its immediate location is also governed by the River Ellen. Roman forts were often situation by a river. If they sat beside a major river such as the Rhine or Danube, the fort was located beside a tributary in order to allow boats to be moored out of the strong flow of water in the main river. When beside a sea, the same rule pertained. Along the east coast of the Black Sea, for example, nearly every fort sat beside one of the rivers flowing into the sea. Maryport is in a similar location. There is thus no reason to invent a special reason for the location of the fort here: it is the most obvious place, on a low hill and beside a tributary flowing into the great inlet of the Irish Sea, the Solway Estuary. In Roman times, however, the river may have taken a slightly different course as it debouched its contents into the sea for Stukeley recorded that the River Ellen 'did not empty itself, formerly, directly into the ocean, as at present, but went northwards under the cliff, till it came under the castle [that is, the fort]: the old channel of it is visible: the sea has eaten away a large quantity of marsh and high ground between it and the castle'. We can now understand that the fort had a slightly different relationship to the river and to the sea than it did 1800 years ago (Figure 15).

At various times, Maryport was the base of Roman army units with exotic names like the First Cohort of Spaniards, the First Cohort of Dalmatians and the First Cohort of Baetasians. These names illustrate the recruiting pattern of the Roman army, but they do not reflect the origin of the soldiers based at

Figure 13. A view of Maryport from the south in the second half of the 19th century. This shows well the whaleback ridge on which the fort sits, the Solway Estuary beyond and Criffel to the left. Reproduced by kind permission of Tyne and Wear Archives and Museums

Maryport. The Baetasians, for example, were a people from what is now the Netherlands. A regiment was raised from their territory shortly after 69 and sent to Britain. Once based in the island, evidence from across the Roman Empire indicates that it would have started recruiting locally, mainly from within Britain, but with some soldiers coming from further afield, but still normally from the north-west provinces of the empire. By the time that the Baetasians arrived at Maryport, probably in about 160, the regiment had been based in the province for nearly 100 years. Generations of new recruits would have joined the regiment, and most would have been British, Gauls or Germans – Labareus, a German, recorded at the fort is likely to have been a soldier though this is not stated on the altar he dedicated.

In spite of knowing the name of several units based at Maryport, we cannot be certain of the name of the fort. This long puzzled antiquarians. They preferred the name *Olenacum*, which is a fort named in the *Notitia Dignitatum*, a list of officials in the Roman Empire dating to about 400. While we now know this is not the case, we remain unsure of the Roman name of Maryport because the *Notitia* is mixed up at this point. The location of the place-name *Alauna* in the *Ravenna Cosmography*, a list of places in the Roman world compiled in Ravenna in the eighth century, best fits Maryport. Seven or eight places called *Alauna*

The Roman army at Maryport

Figure 14. The signpost marks the distance to Rome as well as to Ravenglass and Bowness-on-Solway; in the background is Criffel. Photograph the author

Figure 15. A view of the hill on which sits the Roman fort with the river running at its foot by Joseph Farington, probably painted in the late 18th century; the colour would have been added to this engraving in the late 19th century

are known in Britain and some are associated with rivers, so this would suit Maryport, situated beside the River Ellen. If this is the case, Maryport may be the *Alione* of the *Notitia Dignitatum* where the Third Cohort of Nervians was based. This regiment is not recorded elsewhere at this time, so this is possible. However, not all agree with these arguments. A different perspective was taken by John Mann who argued that Maryport, which he believed played a key role in the coastal system, had been renamed *Praesidium*, which is the Latin name for a fort and in this case presumably an important fort. This argument has no other supporters, and the generally favoured name remains *Alauna*.

The fort

Maryport's Roman fort, the earthworks of which are still visible, is almost square (Figure 16). It measures 139 by 135 m between the crests of its ramparts, providing an internal area of 1.87 ha (4.6 acres). As the fort wall has been robbed out, the crests today represent the surviving tops of the earthen backing to the stone wall surrounding the fort so the enclosure would have been a little larger. Measured over the walls, the dimensions were about 141 by 139 m with an area of 1.99 ha (4.9 acres). This is about the average size of a fort on Hadrian's Wall; Housesteads is just a little larger.

The fort was defended by a stone wall 2 m thick, erected on a foundation of sandstone slabs. A surviving corner of the legionary fortress at York stands 5m (nearly 17 Roman ft) high while the wall at a fort in Germany was 4.5m (15 Roman ft) high to a rampart walk, giving an indication of the height of the fort wall at Maryport. This was backed by an earthen bank of red clay which would

Figure 16. An aerial view of the fort at Maryport looking south-east. Photograph Nick May

have provided support to the wall and aided the movement of soldiers along the fort's rampart. The bank was twice enlarged during the occupation of the fort, achieving a width of 8m. At each internal corner of the fort there was a stone tower, with interval towers between the corners and the gates.

Two ditches are visible round most of the fort defences and this may have been the original number. To the east three ditches were recorded during the 1966 excavation, with a possible fourth under the modern road, cut into the subsoil which varied between clay and sand. The inner ditch was V-shaped and 6.4m wide, the second U-shaped and 4m wide, while the third was W-shaped and 3.8m wide, with the depth reducing from the first to the third ditch. Two features cut into the subsoil beyond the outer ditch suggest earlier activity on the site. There was evidence for re-cutting of the ditches. U-shaped ditches are often indicators of 4th century remodelling of fort defences, and those on the south side are also flat bottomed. Here, at the south-east and south-west corners of the fort, are hints at the former existence of external bastions, a late feature in Roman forts, but known, for example, at Lancaster further down the coast. This work on the defences of the fort in its later years may relate to the threat to the western coast of Britain from the Attacotti and Scots in Ireland recorded in the 360s.

There was a gate in about the middle of each side of the fort (Figure 17). Those to north and south are, however, a little to the west of centre which suggests that the fort faced west towards the sea. This would be appropriate for two Roman writers on military science stated that the fort should face the enemy, and across

Figure 17. These fragments of the north gate are the only visible stones on the site at Maryport today. Photograph the author

Size, 1 ft. 6 in. by 1 ft. 1 in.

Figure 18. This sculptural depiction of a gate was found at Maryport and is presumably of a gate at the fort. The woodcut is reproduced from J. C. Bruce, *Lapidarium Septentrionale*, 901; see Figure 72

the Solway and outside the empire lived the Novantae, an independent people. It is possible that each gate originally had two portals, two roads leading in and out of the fort, which would be normal in the time of the Emperor Hadrian. A sculptural depiction of a gate found at Maryport shows a double-portal gate with an upper storey with five round-headed windows (Figure 18). The arches spring from piers with impost blocks which project forwards and to the side. The gate is similar to that which may be seen today at Housesteads, Birdoswald and Chesters on Hadrian's Wall (Figure 19).

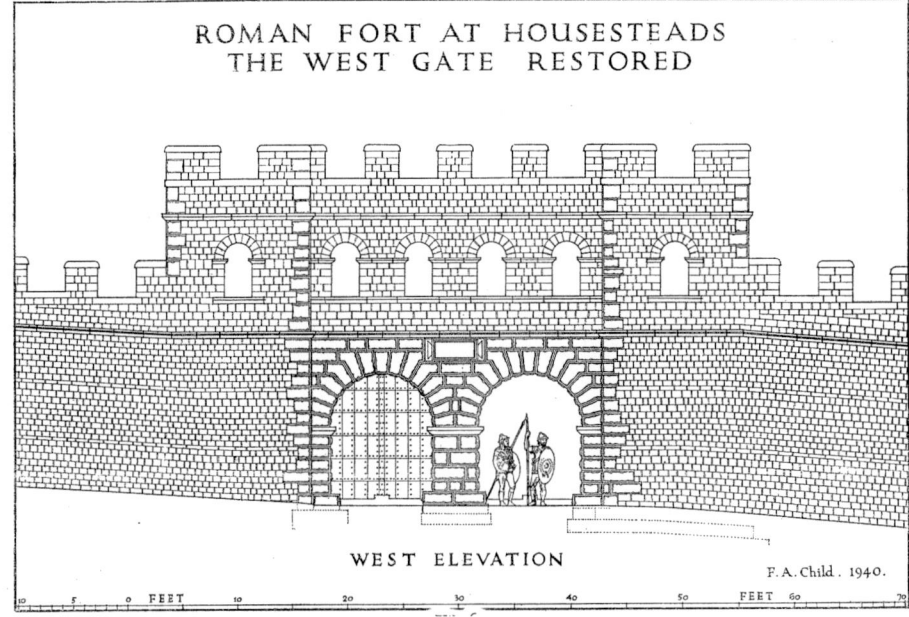

Figure 19. F. A. Child's drawing of the west gate at Housesteads is similar to that on the sculpture at Maryport (*Archaeologia Aeliana* 4 series, 40 (1942) 151)

The Roman fort contained many buildings densely packed into a relatively small area. These were separated by metalled roads passing across the fort from gate to gate. In addition, there was a road running round the interior inside the rampart; this was the intervallum street and at Maryport it was examined in the 1966 excavation on the eastern side.

In the centre of the fort lay the headquarters building. Here were housed the regimental standards, rooms for the clerks, an assembly hall and a courtyard. The strong-room at Maryport, normally placed at the rear of the headquarters building, was examined in 1686 and again in 1766; it was unusually large at 3.20 by 3.66m. This has led to the suggestion that the fort played a special part in the protection of the western seaboard, holding large supplies of money, but in truth that cannot be proved. A well was also recorded which can be ascertained to have been in the courtyard of the headquarters building, as it is, for example, at Chesters on Hadrian's Wall. The house for the commanding officer of the regiment normally was placed to the right of the headquarters building. Here, in 1788, was uncovered part of a bath-house (Figure 20); its approximate location was later supported by the discovery of water-proof wall plaster nearby. The fort's granaries probably lay to the left of the headquarters building. These buildings formed the central range of the fort.

To the front and behind the central range in most forts were barrack-blocks and long narrow buildings usually interpreted as storerooms. Geophysical survey has led to the suggestion of six barrack-blocks to the front of the fort, together with two long narrow buildings, and four to the rear; the two barracks in the north-eastern quarter were partially examined in 1966 (Figure 21). Ten barrack-

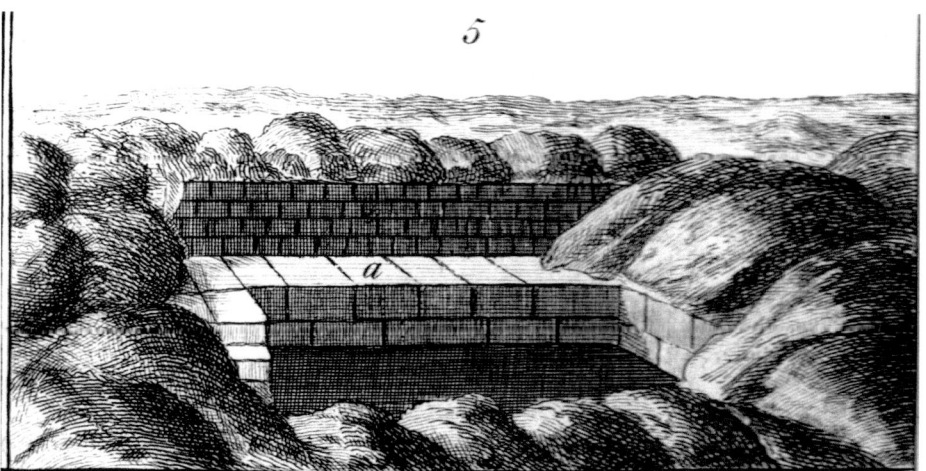

Figure 20. A drawing of part of the commanding officer's bath-house published in *Archaeologia* 10 (1792) opposite p. 140

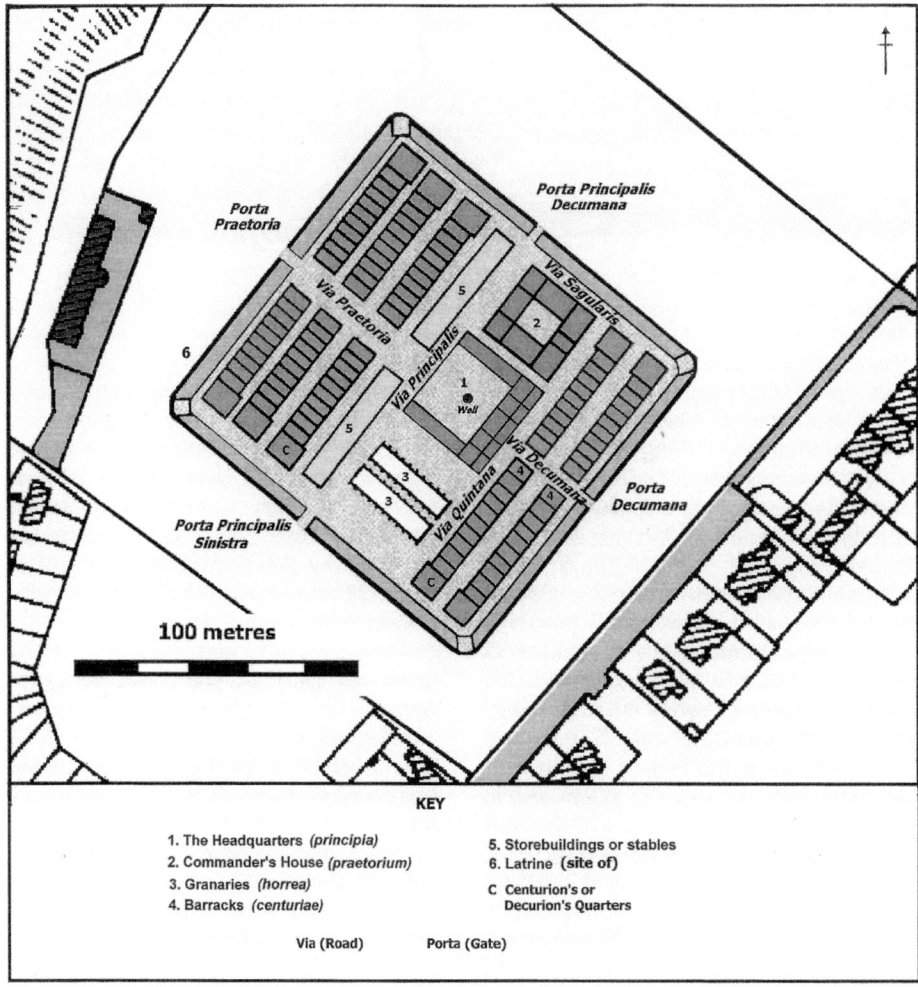

Figure 21. A putative lay-out for the fort by Alan Biggins and David Taylor based on their geophysical survey; see Figure 48

blocks would be appropriate for a regiment containing 480 infantrymen and 128 cavalrymen, such as attested at Maryport, but also for a thousand-strong infantry unit which contained 10 centuries.

Geophysical survey is wonderful at revealing features otherwise invisible below the turf; it cannot, however, date them. Only careful excavation will – with some luck – do that. The 1966 excavation revealed four building phases, which is not surprising in a fort occupied for nearly 300 years. The earliest buildings were presumed to be Hadrianic in date. They were of stone and appear to be barrack-blocks, with part of the centurion's quarters examined. These buildings were re-built, perhaps in the late second century when we know that there was a review of military deployment in northern England. The barrack-blocks were replaced by two narrow buildings. The lower courses were clay-bonded stone walls and it seems likely that the upper parts of the buildings were of timber. These may have been storehouses. Although the date of this work is unknown date, it *may* relate to rebuilding in the fort recorded in 238-44 on an inscription (Figure 27 below). At an even later date, towards the end of the 4th century, the adjacent street, the intervallum road, was repaired, partially overlying the demolished or collapsed corner of one of the narrow buildings. There are also some random post-holes in the area which may be contemporary with this repair. We do not know enough to relate the excavations to the plan created by geophysical survey. We can presume that the buildings on the geophysical plan are unlikely to be the earliest military buildings in the fort as more than two centuries of occupation covered them. Yet a further complication is that the stone walls may hide earlier timber buildings as several forts along the Wall are known to have had such buildings in their primary phase.

Many coins have been found at Maryport, but most of these have been lost. David Shotter has brought together all the evidence and has been able to list 137 coins. These range in date from a single coin of Mark Antony, who died in 30 BC, to the Emperor Honorius who reigned from AD 393 to 423. As Britain separated from the Roman Empire in 409 or 410, the flow of his coins into Britain ceased well before his death.

The number of coins of each reign suggests that a fort was not built at Maryport until at least 100. It was about 103 that the last troops appear to have been withdrawn from north of the Tyne-Solway isthmus and there is a good chance that it was then that a fort was established at Maryport. There is, however, a small fragment of an inscription recording building work on the fort under the Emperor Hadrian and also two fragments of a dedication slab of the First Cohort of Spaniards, based at the fort under Hadrian. As this was the time that Hadrian's Wall was built, and also the fort at Moresby further down the Cumbrian coast (Figure 22),

Figure 22. A building inscription of the Emperor Hadrian found at the fort at Moresby (*RIB* 801); the fragmentary building stone found at Maryport was probably similar

Figure 23. The digger is cleaning what is believed to be the intervallum street of an early fort. To the right of the bucket is a post-Roman field drain and to the right of that the stone foundations of a long Roman building. Photograph Jane Laskey

this would have been an appropriate occasion for the establishment of a fort at Maryport. It remains possible that there was an earlier military installation on the site.

Excavations by Paul Flynn in the field to the south-west of the fort in 2002 and 2005 certainly suggest this. He found evidence of structures which he interpreted as suggesting a smaller, possibly late first century, fort which was then demolished, probably around the time the main fort was constructed under Hadrian (Figure 23). This putative fort would have occupied the area of the level ground beside Pudding Pie Hill. Even this may not be the earliest Roman structure on the site, for the excavations of Ian Haynes and Tony Wilmott discovered a ditch which appears to be part of a Roman temporary camp (Figure 24). This lay north-east of the fort and was aligned north-east to south-west. From its location, it may have been a camp created to hold the soldiers who built the fort.

To return to the visible, and Hadrianic, fort. It is likely that this had reduced occupation when the army moved forward in about 142 to re-occupy southern

Figure 24. The ditch of the Roman camp below the temple looking south, excavated by Ian Haynes and Tony Wilmott

Scotland and build the Antonine Wall; this frontier was abandoned in or soon after 158. At an unknown date in the second half of the second century and the earlier decades of the third century a detachment of the Second and Twentieth Legions came to undertake building work at Maryport (Figure 25). The Twentieth Legion is also recorded by itself (Figure 26). The presence of this legion on several building inscriptions at Mayport is not surprising as the fort appears to have been

Figure 25. A building inscription recording work at Maryport by the Second and Twentieth Legions (*RIB* 852)

Figure 26. A simple record of the Twentieth Legion working at the fort (*RIB* 853)

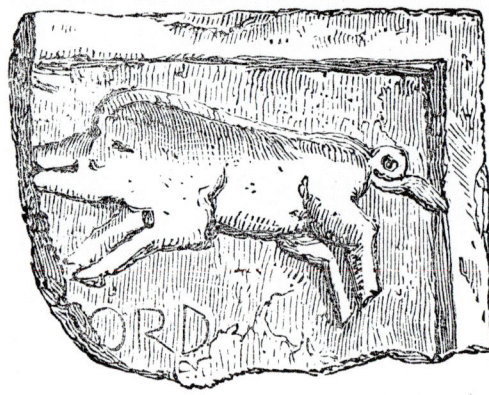

Figure 27. The boar, emblem of the Twentieth Legion, and the possible name of the Emperor Gordian III, reproduced as a woodcut in J. C. Bruce, *Lapidarium Septentrionale*, 892

in the military zone controlled by this legion which was stationed at Chester. One of the latest dated inscriptions from the site is the corner of a stone illustrating a boar, the symbol of the Twentieth Legion. Underneath the board are the letters ...]ORD (Figure 27). This is likely to refer to the Emperor Gordian III, who reigned from 238 to 244; army units often added an emperor's name to their titles, as regiments in the British army do to this day.

The coins indicate occupation continuing at Maryport into the early third century. The civil wars and attacks on the empire in the years from 235 to 284 affected the distribution of coins, but at Maryport the coins point to continuing and probably unbroken activity down to at least 350. Thereafter there are fewer coins into the 370s, but the latest date to the very end of Roman Britain. This conclusion coincides with the evidence provided by the pottery from the 1966 excavation, which suggested unbroken occupation from the Hadrianic period to the late fourth century, a time span of nearly 300 years.

The regiments of Maryport

All our knowledge about the units which were based at Maryport is derived from the extensive series of altars which have been found there over the last

430 years – and more. These provide information about the units which served at Maryport and their commanding officers, but, unfortunately little about the ordinary soldiers.

The First Cohort of Spaniards (cohors I Hispanorum)

This regiment is first attested in Britain in the late first century when it was recorded on an inscription at the fort at Ardoch in modern Perthshire. As the fort was probably only occupied in the 80s, we can tie down its presence there rather tightly. The unit is recorded on diplomas – bronze tablets recording the discharge of soldiers from the army and the award to them (on an individual basis) of Roman citizenship – dating to 98, 103, 105, 122, 124, 127 and 146. On these documents it is always recorded as being a 500-strong infantry unit. Three diplomas dating to 178 record a *cohors I Aelia Hispanorum*. This is presumably the same regiment recorded at Netherby, beyond the western end of Hadrian's Wall, in the year 222, when it was recorded as a thousand-strong mixed unit of infantry and cavalry. Finally, the *Notitia Dignitatum*, a record of all office holders in the Roman Empire dating to about 400, records the *cohors I Hispanorum*, at *Axelodunum*, but, unfortunately, the location of this place is not known. The crunch question is whether this *cohors I Hispanorum* is the same regiment as the *cohors I Aelia Hispanorum*; that, however, does not affect the existence of the cohort at Maryport where its presence is firmly recorded by inscriptions.

The altars of the prefect L. Cammius Maximus all indicate that the First Cohort of Spaniards was a mixed unit of infantry and cavalry 500 men strong, as does that of a prefect whose name is only partially known because

Figure 28. An altar of L. Cammius Maximus recording the fact that the First Cohort of Spaniards had a cavalry component indicated by EQ in the bottom line (*RIB* 828)

Figure 29. Peter Connolly's painting of a cavalryman, left, and infantryman. Reproduced by kind permission of the Römisch-Germanischen Zentral-museum, Mainz

his altar is lost (Figure 28). Such regiments contained 480 infantry and 128 cavalry so the paper strength of the unit would be 608. The infantry was organised in six centuries each 80 men strong while the 128 cavalrymen were divided into four troops (Figure 29). The full strength of the regiment including the officers would be 619.

The inscriptions are not without their own problems for they record two different titles for the commanding officer. In two or three cases, the commander was a tribune and in the other four he was a prefect. A prefect normally commanded a 500-strong regiment and a tribune a thousand-strong unit. The implication is that at some point when the regiment was at Maryport it was either increased or reduced in size. There has been considerable discussion of this question, which is still without resolution. The size and postulated plan of the fort would better suit a five-hundred strong regiment than one with a strength of a thousand men.

The most famous tribune at Maryport was Marcus Maenius Agrippa (Figure 30). An inscription erected in his home town of Camerinum in Italy, about 150 km north-east of Rome, records his distinguished career. He was not a top flight Roman aristocrat, but a member of the next tier down, termed the knights, though we might call them the gentry. He had started his career in the army as commander of a small auxiliary unit 500 strong and he steadily rose through the imperial service to end his career as procurator of Britain, that is, as the senior financial officer of the province, almost at the very pinnacle of the hierarchy. His career inscription proudly recorded that his son became a senator. It also states that he had been host to the Emperor Hadrian and had served on the expedition to Britain. Unfortunately, the date of neither is given. The preferred date for the expedition is Hadrian's visit in 122, though this is not without its detractors, and perhaps he was host to his emperor in 127 when Hadrian toured the part of Italy containing Camerinum. So, it looks as though he commanded at Maryport in the years following 122, returning in time to welcome Hadrian to his home town.

Figure 30. An altar dedicated by M. Maenius Agrippa; this was presumably the first of the annual altars that he dedicated to Jupiter as he named the unit as well as himself (*RIB* 823)

The second tribune is Caius Caballius Priscus (Figure 31). We know nothing about him, though another soldier with the same name had a link with Verona in northern Italy.

The prefect Lucius Antistius Lupus Verianus recorded on his inscription that he came from Sicca in North Africa, the modern Le Kef in western Tunisia (Figure 37 below). Helstrius Novellus, also a prefect, is otherwise anonymous (Figure 32). The other two prefects, Cammius Maximus and Censorinus Cornelianus, are discussed below.

Finally, we should note amongst possible commanders of this regiment Caius Cornelius Peregrinus (Figures 33 and 3). His regiment is not named, but he was a tribune and the First Cohort of Spaniards is the only unit based at Maryport known to have had tribunes as its commanding officers. Peregrinus came from

| Figure 31. An altar dedicated by C. Caballius Priscus (*RIB* 817) | Figure 32. The altar to Jupiter dedicated by Helstrius Novellus (*RIB* 822) |

Saldae in the province of Mauretania Caesariensis in modern Algeria where he was a town councillor.

Fifteen inscriptions record the tribunes and prefects of the First Cohort of Spaniards. To these we can add: Cornelius Peregrinus; an altar which bears the name of the regiment but not the commanding officer; a third which has lost its face but can be identified as belonging to the regiment on the basis of the motifs on its top as these are associated only with the First Cohort of Spaniards (these are discussed below); a fragment bearing the letter S preceded by the upper serif of I, and in the style of the lettering of the First Cohort of Spaniards, found in 2012. Seventeen of these altars are dedicated to Jupiter and if we add the presence of Cornelius Peregrinus, and look at the evidence in a simplistic way, there is one altar for every year of the reign of Hadrian from his visit to Britain in 122 through to his death in 138.

Figure 33. The altar dedicated by C. Cornelius Peregrinus (*RIB* 812). The stone was found in the north-west corner of the fort before 1599. It is decorated with a human bust and animal heads and the inscription is flanked by fluted columns; see Figure 3

Figure 34. This unusual stone was dedicated by P. Postumius Acilianus, prefect of the First Cohort of Delmatians (*RIB* 833). The rosette is repeated on the sides and the back of the stone, which appears to have been designed to carry a statue.

The First Cohort of Dalmatians (cohors I Delmatarum)

This regiment was raised in Dalmatia before the reign of the Emperor Claudius (41-54), and then stationed in Germany. The unit may have formed part of the army of invasion of Britain in 43, and if not was here soon afterwards. It is recorded in Britain on diplomas issued in 122, 124 and 135. It was stationed at Maryport in the reign of the Emperor Antoninus Pius (138-161) and was recorded building at Chesters on Hadrian's Wall later in the second century.

Only two prefects of this unit are known, Lucius Caecilius Vegetus and Paulus Postumius Acilianus (Figure 34). We know nothing about the former, but the latter may be the descendant of a freedman of Postumius Acilianus of Cordova in southern Spain, a procurator under Trajan. Our Acilianus appears on two inscriptions which both mention the Emperor Antoninus Pius (138-61). One inscription at Maryport recording this emperor does not mention one of his titles, Father of his Country, granted in 139, so unless this is an accidental omission we can date the inscription closely.

The First Cohort of Baetasians (cohors I Baetasiorum)

The Emperor Nero committed suicide – with some help – in 68 and over the next year or so there were four emperors, and a major revolt in the Lower Rhine region. In the aftermath of this rebellion, the First Cohort of Baetasians was raised from the area of the uprising, and sent to Britain with the new governor Petillius Cerialis in 71. The regiment appears on diplomas issued in 103, 122, 124 and 135. It appears to have been part of the army which invaded Scotland in 139/40 at the beginning of the reign of the Emperor Antoninus Pius because when it erected a building stone at its base at Bar Hill on the new frontier, the Antonine Wall, it recorded that its members have been awarded the Roman citizenship usually given for meritorious conduct in battle. When the Antonine Wall was abandoned in 158 or soon afterwards, the regiment was posted to Maryport. In the early third century, it moved to the opposite corner of the country, the fort at Reculver in Kent, where it remained until the end of Roman Britain.

Again, only two prefects of this unit are known, Ulpius Titianus and Titus Attius Tutor, a native of Solva in Noricum where his career inscription was erected (Figure 35). After serving as a town councillor of Solva (in modern Austria) he entered the imperial service as commanding officer of the First

Figure 35. An altar dedicated by T. Attius Tutor (*RIB* 838)

Cohort of Baetasians. He then moved to Aquincum, modern Budapest, where he served as a tribune in the legion based there. His next move was to Dacia, modern Romania, where he held two posts as commander of cavalry regiments, the second in charge of a thousand-strong cavalry unit, the most prestigious appointment in the hierarchy in this particular branch of the imperial service.

Careers in the emperor's service

The inscriptions at Maryport record officers travelling to the fort from many places to take up their commands (Figure 36). They came from today's Italy, France, Austria, North Africa (Figure 37) and possibly Spain.

The command at Maryport was the lowest rung in the hierarchy for men of their class, that is town councillors and Roman knights, but many went on to service elsewhere, usually at the other end of the empire from Maryport, that is, Judaea, Dacia and the Danubian provinces. Some did well in the imperial service. Attius Tutor rose to the command of the most senior type of auxiliary unit. Maenius Agrippa was promoted even further, reached almost the top of the tree for any equestrian officer, as procurator of a senior province, namely Britain.

Some inscriptions at Maryport usefully record additional information about later appointments. Lucius Cammius Maximus had squeezed into the end of his dedication that he was tribune of the Eighteenth Cohort of Volunteers (Figure 38). This unit was stationed in Upper Pannonia on the Middle Danube (modern Austria) between 138 and 154. It seems likely that Maximus was recording his promotion to this unit based half-way across the Empire. It is possible that he was moving closer to home for a man of this name was a town councillor of Solva in Noricum, the neighbouring province to Upper Pannonia (Solva is in the southern part of the Austrian province of Styria).

One of the most frustrating inscriptions is that erected by Marcus Censorius Cornelianus, a native of Nemausus, Nîmes, in modern France (Figure 39). This records that he was a centurion in the Tenth Legion Fretensis, which was based in Judaea. Like Cammius Maximus, he was probably recording his promotion to the centurionate because appointments in the other direction are not known at this time. A possible occasion for this promotion, and move right across the empire, was when Julius Severus, governor of Britain, was sent to the East to take command of the Roman army against the Jewish rebels in what is known as the Bar Kokhba uprising which broke out in 132. Severus may have taken Cornelianus with him, and in turn the commander may have been accompanied by part of his regiment. A reduction in the strength of the First Cohort of Spaniards remaining at Maryport would then have been the occasion for the demotion in the status of its commanding officer from tribune to prefect.

Frontiers of the Roman Empire

Roman provinces and frontiers in the Hadrianic period

Figure 36. A map of the Roman empire showing the provinces which were the homes to the commanders at Maryport and where they went on to serve. Copyright the author

Figure 37. L. Antistius Lupus Verianus states that his city of origin was Sicca in North Africa (*RIB* 816)

Figure 38. The altar dedicated to Jupiter by L. Cammius Maximus is unfortunately damaged, but it does record his promotion to the Eighteenth Cohort of Volunteers (*RIB* 827)

While the governor, Julius Severus, may have picked out Cornelianus in this way, the appointment would have had to be approved by the emperor. We are informed that Maenius Agrippa was the host of Hadrian, but the emperor would have had knowledge of all the other officers serving at Maryport for he appointed them, or approved their appointment. The letters of the Younger Pliny also demonstrate that having friends in the right places helped because they could put in a good word for you. And having the cheek to ask for a post sometimes brought its own reward. This equally applied to the soldiers in the unit. Interesting relevant letters survive in the eastern provinces of the empire. One soldier complained that he had not been given a good enough reference for the regiment he wished to join, another went to the commander of his legion to ask for a promotion; as Claudius Terentianus wrote to his father, 'nothing can be done without money, nor will letters of recommendation be of any use, unless a man helps himself'.

The altars at Maryport have a particular and signal contribution to our understanding of the Roman army. There are 18 – probably 19 – altars dedicated to Jupiter by the commanders of the First Cohort of Spaniards. While the religious significance of the dedications will be discussed later, at this point we merely need to note that each altar probably represents a year in the life of the cohort. Thus, we can divide the number of altars by the number of commanders to reach a rough average for each officer of three years at the fort. Every book on the Roman army will quote that figure and in each case the statement is based on the evidence at Maryport.

Soldiers

We have little information on the literally thousands of soldiers who must have served at Maryport. The tombstone of Julius Marinus, a centurion (called *ordinarius* on the inscription) – the

Figure 39. This altar erected by M. Censorius Cornelianus records both his transfer to the Tenth Legion Fretensis based in Judaea and that his home was Nemausus, modern Nîmes (*RIB* 814)

commander of a century of 80 men and, as a professional soldier, one of the most important men in the regiment – records that he lived for 40 years (Figure 40). Most soldiers entered the army between 18 and 21 years of age. Some sought, and obtained, posts which gave them immunity from fatigues and then, perhaps, promotion to a post earning extra pay. A small number, usually after about 13 or 14 years' service, achieved promotion to centurion. While ordinary soldiers had to retire after 25 years, there was no retirement age for centurions; one is recorded having served 61 years in the army. Centurions were allowed to marry so it is likely that Maritima, who erected the tombstone, is the wife of Julius Marinus.

Figure 40. The tombstone of Julius Marinus, recording his rank, *ordinarius* (centurion), at the end of the 2nd line and age 40 (*RIB* 858)

Julius Civilis was a *optio*, that is, the second in command of a century. A stone found in a house in the extra-mural settlement examined by Robinson in 1880 bears the figure of a man holding a spear scratched on it and the letters SIG or SEG (or SEC). This has been variously interpreted as being an abbreviation of *signifer*, that is, a standard bearer, or the god Segomo.

The status of other men is not clear: Labareus a German recorded on an altar; Marcus Septimius, Julius Senecianus, Julius Simplex, Aelius Sacas[... and Vireius Paul[... on tombstones; Quintus, father of Hermione; Moriregis, who lived for 70 years and whose tombstone was erected by his sons and heirs; Tirunc(ulus); and a man born in Galatia in modern Turkey and who also died there but who wished to be buried in the tomb of his father presumably at Maryport (Figure 41). Possibly all were soldiers, and most likely the last two. The name Karus was deeply scratched onto a samian bowl found in the rubbish tip beside the cliff top in 1880, but it is not known whether this was a soldier or civilian. The name D]OCCEI appears on the side of an amphora, a large wine jar, but it is not clear

Figure 41. The tombstone of a man from Galatia, which can be read in the 3rd line (*RIB* 864)

whether this was the name of the merchant, the manufacturer of the vessel, or its owner.

We know the name of two specialists at Maryport. One was Aulus Egnatius Pastor who erected a dedication slab in Greek to Asclepius, the Greek god of medicine and healing, and was therefore probably the regimental doctor, and a soldier (Figure 42). The other was Indutius, whose name appears on a tile he made; the name suggests that he was German, or of German descent (Figure 43).

Figure 42. A dedication in Greek to Asclepius by A. Egnatius Pastor, presumably the regimental doctor (*RIB* 808)

Figure 43. This tile bears the inscription, COH I HISPA|INDVTIVSFEC, The First Cohort of Spaniards, Indutius made this (*RIB* 2474)

Chapter 3

The extra-mural community

One may trace many square plots of the houses, and of the streets, paved with broad flagstones, that are visible worn with use. William Stukeley

A Roman fort was the centre of a large community. A Roman army – any army – will always attract hangers on. In the account of his conquest of Gaul in the 50s BC Julius Caesar mentioned camp followers several times, and he made them sleep outside his camp. A couple of generations before, a new general, Scipio Aemilianus, arrived in Spain to take command of the army there. There are no less than five sources for one of his first actions, which was to eject 2000 prostitutes from the camp at Numantia. Other camp followers included wives and families, traders and soothsayers ... and slaves. The number of camp followers could be as large as the army itself.

So, we must imagine that when each unit arrived at Maryport to take up residence in the fort, it arrived with a long train of what we might call the military community. Many came because they had nowhere else to go. These included the families of soldiers. Although soldiers were not allowed to marry according to Roman law until well into the 3rd century, many contracted unions with women who became, in modern parlance, their partners, possibly marrying them according to local custom. Such relationships usually did not occur until the soldier had been promoted in some way and was leading a more stable existence than an ordinary private. Although the Roman army did not acknowledge such unions while the soldier was in service, their existence was accepted when he retired and was awarded the 'right of marriage with the wife they had when citizenship was given to them'. One result of this arrangement was that the army did not have to pay the transport costs of the soldiers' families when the unit moved on, though whether that was the reason for the ban on marriage according to Roman law is not known.

If a soldier had a partner, he might also have children, and, since many soldiers were the sons of soldiers – 'born in the camp' – they might also have a mother, sister(s), mother-in-law and so on. At about the time that the fort at Maryport was built, the Emperor Hadrian affirmed that while children who were born and acknowledged during military service were not the legitimate heirs of the fathers, they should be allowed to claim possession of their father's property. Again, this was the state recognising the realities of life.

Roman women at Maryport

Lindsay Allason-Jones has studied the women of Roman Britain and written about those who lived at Maryport. Unfortunate only four women are known by name, …]iana Hermione, Maritima, Julia Martina and Sotera. Rather surprisingly in view of this paucity of names, Hermione is recorded twice. It is probable that one of her altars was dedicated to the goddess Juno, though the name only survives in part on the stone, and another to the Valour of the Emperor, both recording that she was the daughter of Quintus. The recipients of the dedications, and the formality of her name, which includes that of her father, suggest that she was a member of the army community, almost certainly the daughter of an officer. Her Greek name is interesting, and hints that her father may have been a doctor like Egnatius Pastor.

Sotera was the wife of Julius Senecianus and although her husband's second name is frequently found in the north-western provinces of the empire, Sotera is a Greek name. Allason-Jones speculates that she was a slave and given the name Sotera, following the fashion for slaves to have Greek names, and later freed to marry Julius Senecianus.

Maritima erected the tombstone of the centurion Julius Marinus who died at the age of 40. It might be expected that she was the wife of Marinus, but she could have been his slave – a sister or mother might be expected to have his name so she is unlikely to have been a blood relative. Maritima's single name suggests that she was not a freeborn citizen.

Our last female member of the military community is Julia Martina who died at the age of 12 years, 3 months and 22 days (Figure 44). Her name demonstrates that she was a Roman citizen. No family member is mentioned on the tombstone. We should also note Ingenuus, another juvenile, who died aged ten and was commemorated by his father Julius Simplex, and also that of Luca, whose gender is uncertain.

It would not be surprising if there were many women who were Roman citizens at Maryport for the citizenship was given to the soldiers based at the fort when they retired. Although their wives were not made citizens, this privilege was

Figure 44. The tombstone of Julia Martina (*RIB* 866),
reproduced as a woodcut in J. C. Bruce,
Lapidarium Septentrionale, 879

extended to their children, and to their posterity. In 140, for a reason we do not understand, the rules were changed and thereafter the grant of citizenship ceased to apply retrospectively to existing children but was only extended to children born after the end of military service.

Two items of sculpture provide some information on the dress of the women of Maryport. They are very worn, suggesting that they stood for many years in the exposed conditions of Maryport's whaleback hill. One woman wore the ungirt Gallic tunic and cloak around her shoulders which was the typical dress of women in the north-western provinces of the empire from the late first century to the late third century (Figure 45). She holds objects in her hands, which are difficult to identify but may be a purse or a mirror as on other tombstones.

Figure 45. A female figure wearing an ungirt Gallic tunic and cloak around the shoulders, the typical dress of women in the north-western Roman provinces from the late 1st to the late 3rd centuries

A second lady wears a foot-length girt Roman tunic and palla draped over her left shoulder and upper arm; this may suggest that she was a priestess (Figure 46). She appears to have her hair worn open, which is only ever seen in mourning scenes, which would be appropriate for a tombstone.

Female objects are few, indeed almost non-existent, just one bracelet being identified as female, but this reflects the number of objects from the site generally. The fragment of a glass bangle may have belonged to woman, or a child, but it is possible that such objects were used to decorate horses (Figure 47).

One group of people are not certainly represented at Maryport, slaves. Slavery was endemic in the Roman world. Soldiers owned slaves, either as individuals or as part of a group such as a barrack room, and occasionally they appear on tombstones, even holding the spears of their cavalry masters. Households in the civilian community would have had slaves, rather as many middle-class houses in the 19th century had at least one servant.

THE EXTRA-MURAL COMMUNITY 47

Figure 46. A female figure wearing a foot-length girt Roman tunic and palla draped over her left shoulder and upper arm, and the woodcut of the same tombstone published in J. C. Bruce, *Lapidarium Septentrionale*, 890

Figure 47. A fragment of a glass bangle found at Maryport. The fragment measures 23mm by 8mm and is reproduced here at twice the actual size.

Geophysical survey

Until this century, little was known about the settlement outside the fort walls at Maryport. Early visitors had recorded buildings, and excavations in the 1870s and '80s had unearthed the remains of a few stone structures. Aerial survey had produced evidence for roads and ditches. Our knowledge was, however, revolutionised by the geophysical survey carried out by Alan Biggins and David Taylor between 2000 and 2004 at the request of the Senhouse Museum Trust (Figure 48). All parties were keen to extend the survey well beyond the fragmentary known remains so that we could be sure that we had found everything for which evidence survived in the vicinity of the fort. The sea provided a boundary to the west and the valley of the Barney Gill to the east. To the south lay the modern town of Maryport and to the north we extended as far as Milefortlet 23, a third of a Roman mile north of the fort.

The resulting map – the word 'plan' does not convey the extent of the remains – was remarkable. Revealed was an extra-mural settlement larger than the fort, extending twice the width of the fort to the north-east, with stone houses clearly visible bounded by a bewildering array of ditches. This was, and remains, one of the most extensive geophysical surveys outside any fort anywhere in the Roman Empire.

In their report on their discoveries, Alan Biggins and David Taylor set down the information they had brought to life. Immediately beyond the northern ditches of the fort, the buildings cluster in a thick band along the whole length of the fort and even round the corners. They noted that the line of the road leading from the north gate of the fort continued onwards with stone strip buildings fronting the road on each side. The buildings continue for 350m from the fort, though with their density declining. Many buildings were large, 7 to 11m wide, often with smaller structures to their rear. The more normal width for the buildings was up to 7m, typical of similar settlements along Hadrian's Wall.

The lower courses of these buildings were of stone, but it is not known whether the upper parts were of stone or were half-timbered. Certainly, they would have required a considerable quantity of timber in order to span the 7m width, and create the roofs, though it is probable that the wider buildings would have had internal supports following an aisled construction technique. The stone, usually the local red sandstone, was presumably obtained locally, perhaps from the cliff where it was quarried in the 19th century.

These buildings, and the plots in which they sat, can be planned, but we have to use our imagination in most cases to determine what happened within them. In

The extra-mural community   49

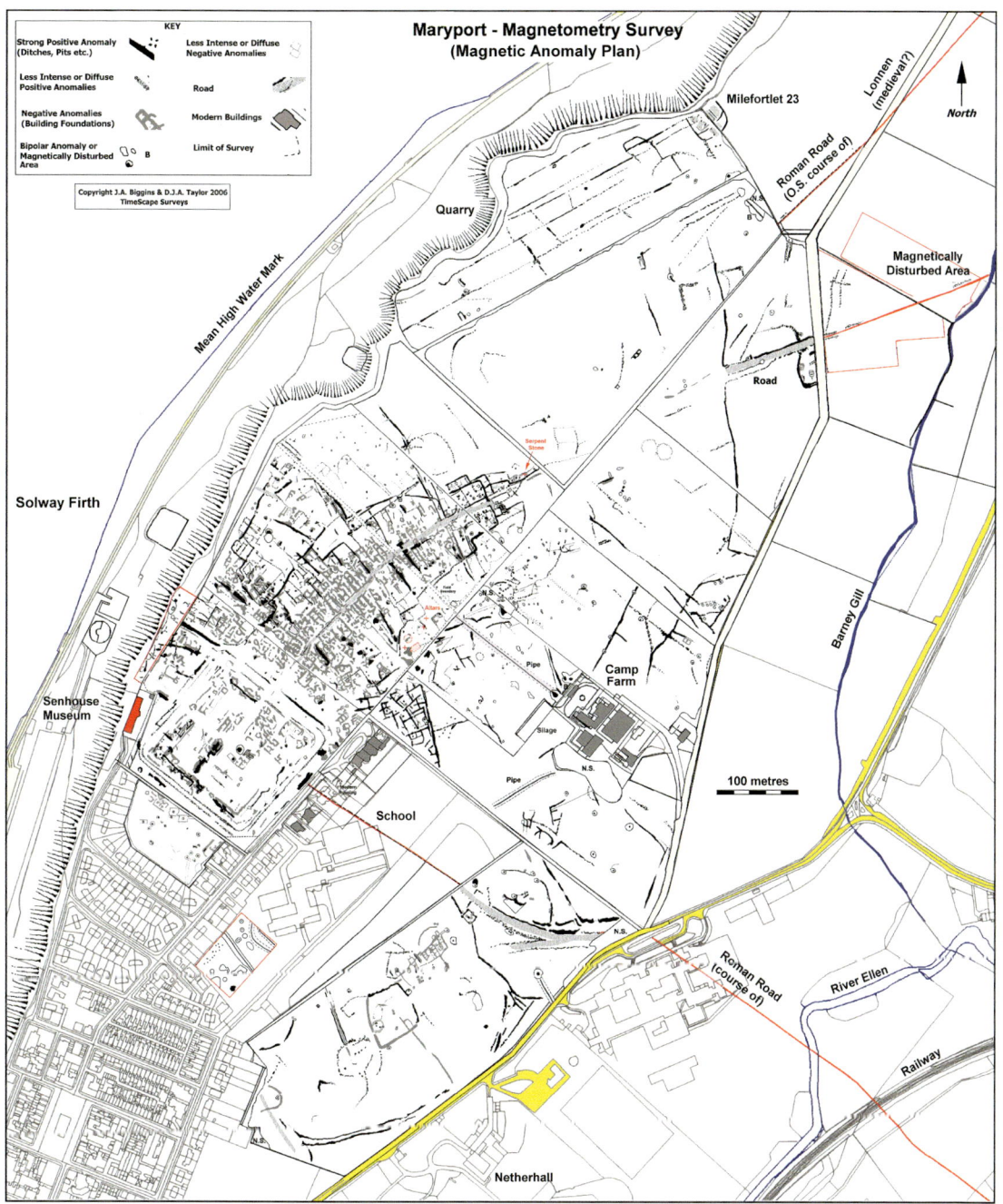

Figure 48. The geophysical survey undertaken by Alan Biggins and David Taylor

only a few instances can a function for a building be suggested. One building, for example, was about 26 m long and about 11m wide with four possible buttresses on one side, and with stone supports for a raised floor recognisable; this was interpreted as a granary – two granaries have been identified in the Roman town at Corbridge.

A feature of the extra-mural settlement were the ditches which surround most of the buildings and their plots. Many could represent field boundaries, some might be for defence, or simply administrative and legal convenience. It would appear that in certain places the stone buildings overlay ditches. North of the extra-mural settlement, the fields are between 13 and 17m wide and about 60 m from front to back. Does this indicate the use of the building as a farm house, or was it simply that many inhabitants grew – or raised – their own food? Some of the boundaries appear to be continuous on both sides of the road and Biggins and Taylor suggested that in these cases they could predate the road.

Buildings in the settlement

In his wide-ranging investigation of the site in 1880, Joseph Robinson discovered many features in the area to the north of the fort. His first work had a rescue element about it as a quarry had been opened up to the west of the fort in order to obtain stone for the new dock. Here Robinson found the remains of a building, now a jumble of dressed stones. His citing of heavy foundation stones and fine building blocks suggest that this had been a substantial building. He also found a large area of 'rich black layer of earth' containing much pottery, a coin, quantities of slate, roofing and flooring tiles, and building stones; it seems probable that this was a Roman rubbish tip.

Robinson's more productive work was elsewhere in the area north of the fort (Figure 49). He started to uncover the main road on 12 April, and recorded its width as 21 ft (6.4m). He discovered a large stone conduit which he concluded carried water under the road. He uncovered walls, one at least 53 ft (16m) long, which he assumed formed part of a house. He noted artefacts, including a ribbed green, glass bead. On 17 April he moved northwards and found the Serpent Stone and other remains in its vicinity. Ploughing brought the work here to an end on 27 April. On the next day he returned to the main area of buildings, discovering an altar and the temple, and then the adjacent circular building. Another altar followed at about seven o'clock in the morning of 3 May, then two heads, fortuitously uncovered in the presence of Mrs Senhouse and Dr J. Collingood Bruce. Sculpture, a small household altar, the fragment of another altar, and coins were recovered. There is a breathlessness about Robinson's report, one discovery follows closely on another as he moves round the site. At

THE EXTRA-MURAL COMMUNITY   51

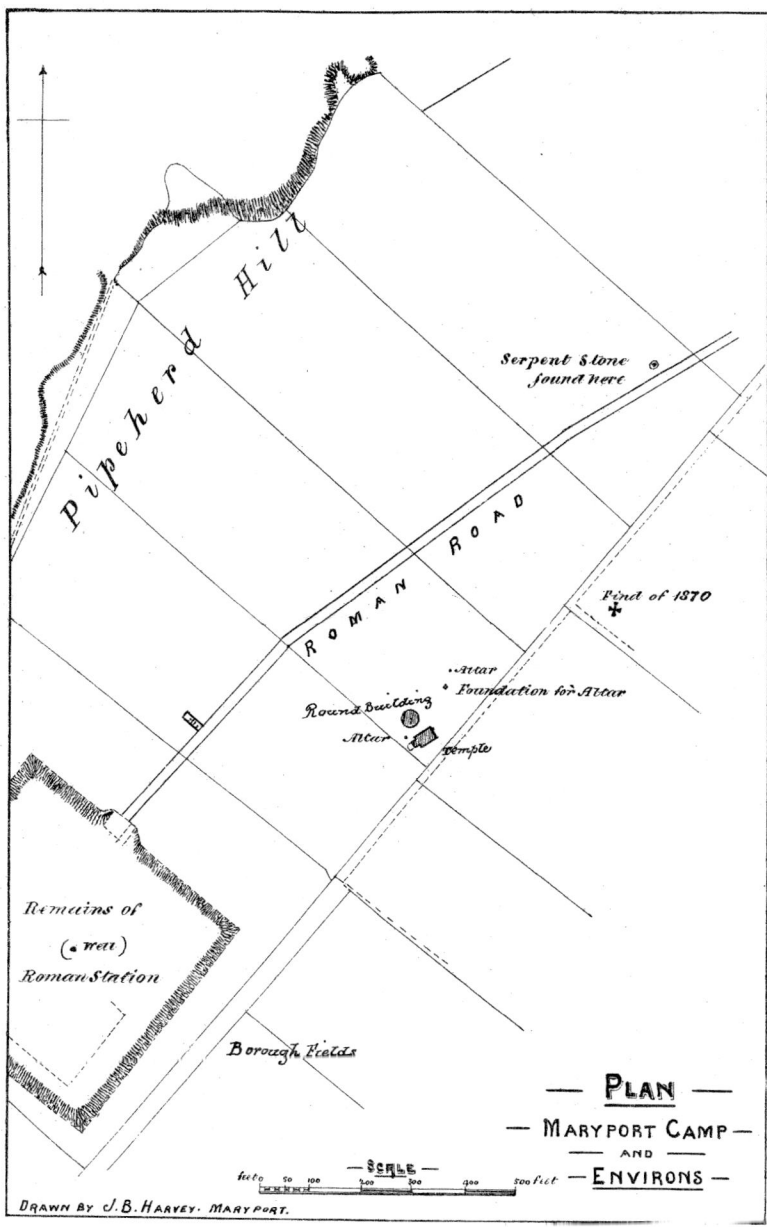

Figure 49. Joseph Robinson's plan of his discoveries.
The modern field pattern was established in the 19th century

the same time, other excavations were in progress leading to the uncovering of 'a breadth of sixty-three feet [19m] of pavement', but he does not tell us where; 'out of another was dug a quantity of iron debris, mixed with small coal' ... 'It

FOUNDATIONS NEAR ROMAN CAMP, MARYPORT.

Figure 50. The house excavated by Joseph Robinson

was impossible to dig in this part without finding remains of houses'. Locals helped, including a local boy who found an item of sculpture apparently lying on the ground.

Robinson's final area of investigation was the field directly to the north-east of the fort where, again, he found walls, pavements, pottery and so on. This time he decided to excavate a complete house (Figure 50). This lay on the seaward side of the road. It measured 12.34 by 5.16m, with the walls 762mm thick. The landward side of the building was complete, but 2.13m from the ends of the side walls at the seaward side of the building lay a cross wall. Robinson could not determine whether this formed the end of a building 13.72m long, not least because the character of the stones was different and only one course survived. He also recorded that he found no mortar in the building, nor in the surrounding area. A door opened about half-way along the south-westerly wall, with two large flags to the outside. Alongside the building was a passage. The floor of the building consisted of flags, mainly round the entrance, large stones and gravel. A row of upright flags was interpreted as an internal subdivision. Slates were found inside the building, several with holes in them for pinning to the timber frame of the roof, in some cases the nails surviving attached to the slates. Other

Figure 51. The house excavated by Oxford Archaeology North looking north-west.
Copyright Oxford Archaeology

discoveries were parts of one or more glass jars, pottery sherds, parts of the lower stone of a quern, a coin of Faustina, the wife of the Emperor Antoninus Pius, some human bones, and the stone bearing the letters SIG or SEG.

In 2013 and 2014 Oxford Archaeology North undertook the excavation of a single building plot, in the extra-mural settlement (Figures 51 and 52). The building lay on the seaward side of the main road running through the settlement. Here were long, narrow building plots running out from the road. A stone building measuring about 20 by 5m was exposed. The building appears to have contained a row of three rooms, the front one opening onto the road. This room had clay floors; the middle room had a floor of flag-stones and yielded some evidence for smithing. This was not the first building on the site as traces of earlier activity

Figure 52. Chain mail dating to the 2nd or 3rd century found during the Oxford Archaeology North excavation

were visible. Behind the house were possible wells or cisterns, the area being bounded by a V-shaped ditch. The house seems to have been abandoned in the late third century.

Administration

The survival of an altar dedicated to the god Belatucadrus at Maryport is of more than local interest. Belatucadrus appears to have been the main god of the tribe or state known as the Carvetii who occupied the Eden valley running south from Carlisle. Their main town was probably at Carlisle, but they may have spread as far east as Carvoran on the watershed between the Solway basin and the Tyne basin, and as far south as Middleton in Lonsdale where a milestone records the more-or-less correct distance from Carlisle, 53 Roman miles. The dedication at Maryport suggests that the territory of the Carvetii may have embraced the Solway plain.

A senator of the city, Flavius Martius, died at Old Penrith aged 45. It is not clear whether the senators of the *civitas Carvetiorum* would have held jurisdiction over the civilians resident at Maryport. Nevertheless, it is likely that they had their own self-governing rights, as did the civilians at Housesteads and Vindolanda on Hadrian's Wall and those outside the fort at Carriden at the eastern end of the Antonine Wall. The relationship between the army and these self-governing civilian communities remains a matter of speculation.

Chapter 4

Religion at Maryport

Iupiter Optimus Maximus (Jupiter, Best and Greatest)

Eighteen hundred and seventy was a year of international importance for Maryport. In April, a ploughman hit a stone object which led to further investigations and to the discovery of 17 Roman altars buried in a series of pits on the summit of the whaleback ridge on which sits the Roman fort (Figures 53, 54 and 55). Many of the altars were dedicated to Jupiter, the chief god of the Roman Pantheon, the Roman equivalent of the Greek Zeus. Other discoveries bring the total number of altars dedicated to Jupiter to 23 or 24.

The inscriptions on the altars follow a distinct pattern. This can readily be seen on those of two commanding officers of the First Cohort of Spaniards, Maenius Agrippa and Caballius Priscus. In each case four altars survive. One gives the name of the regiment and that of the commanding officer, in that order; the other three only carry the name of the commander (Figures 56 and 57). The conclusion would appear to be that in his first year, a new commanding officer dedicated an altar on behalf of himself and his unit while in subsequent years he dedicated by himself, the name of the unit being understood. But what was the occasion?

Surviving letters written by the Younger Pliny, when governor of Bithynia and Pontus (in modern Turkey), to the Emperor Trajan at the beginning of the second century provide important information. Following the renewal of the annual oath of loyalty to the emperor on 3 January 113 (Tacitus states that the event occurred on 1 January in 69 when Galba was emperor), Pliny wrote, 'we have discharged the vows, sir, renewed last year, amidst general enthusiasm and rejoicing, and have made those for the coming year, the soldiers and provincials

 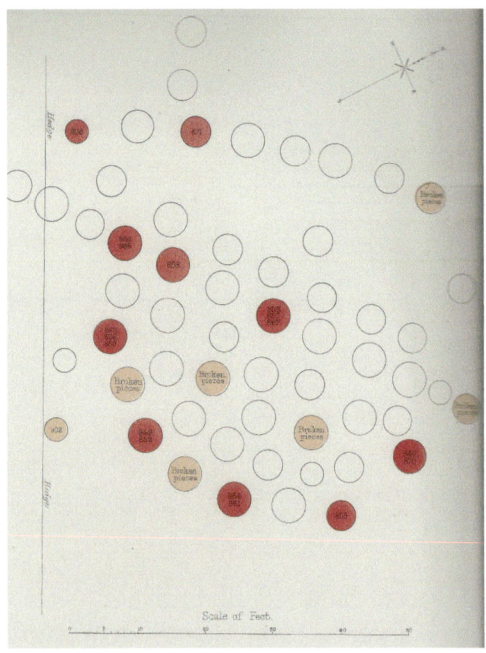

Figure 53. J. Collingwood Bruce at the entrance to the keep of Newcastle castle with a sculpture of Victory found at Housesteads; Bruce travelled to Maryport to record the altars. Copyright Society of Antiquaries of Newcastle upon Tyne and the Great North Museum Hancock

Figure 54. J. C. Bruce's plan of the altar pits; the excavations of Ian Haynes and Tony Wilmott demonstrated that this is not accurate

Figure 55. The altar pits as revealed by the excavations of Ian Haynes and Tony Wilmott

Figure 56. This altar by C. Caballius Priscus records the name of the regiment he commanded (*RIB* 817)

Figure 57. This altar, also dedicated by C. Caballius Priscus, states only his name with the name of his regiment understood (*RIB* 818)

competing with one another in loyal demonstrations. We have prayed to the gods to preserve you and the state in prosperity and safety, and to show you the favour you deserve for your many great virtues, and above all for your sanctity, reverence and piety'. Trajan replied, 'I am glad to hear from your letter, my dear Pliny, that the soldiers and the provincials, amidst general rejoicing have discharged under your direction their vows to the immortal gods for my safety, and have renewed them for the coming year'.

Later that month, Pliny wrote again to his emperor, 'we have celebrated with due solemnity the day [28 January] on which the security of the human race was happily transferred to your care, commending our public vows and thanksgiving to the gods to whom we owe your authority', and Trajan responded, 'I was glad to hear from your letter that the day of my accession was celebrated under your direction by the soldier and provincials with due rejoicing and solemnity'.

There was one other occasion so marked, the birthday of the emperor, in this case 18 September. In 112 Pliny wrote, 'it is my prayer, sir, that this birthday and many others to come will bring you the greatest happiness, and that in health and strength you may add to the immortal fame and glory of your reputation by every new achievement'. Trajan's response was as courteous as ever, 'I write in acknowledgement of your prayers, my dear Pliny, that I may spend many birthdays made happy by the continued prosperity of our country'.

Florid these may be, but they are enormously useful in providing an insight into state ceremonies, the relations between emperor and governor, and they also imply a considerable and continuing flow of letters from governors to emperors, which we know was through the imperial postal system – Pliny in another letter offers an insight into this because he provided a pass to his young wife to visit her ill grandfather and then sought retrospective approval from the emperor.

The nature of the ceremony is of particular interest. Roman religion operated in a different way from many modern religions in which a vital element is praise of God. In Roman religion, the person, or in this case persons, sought a bargain with the gods. He took a vow that if a particular god or goddess would favour or protect him in a particular circumstance he would do something in return such as sacrifice an animal or erect an altar to the deity; it was essentially a bargain. So, the soldiers in Pliny's letters discharged the vows made the previous year – presumably by the dedication of an altar – and prayed to the gods to preserve the emperor for another year. The question for us, however, is which particular event – or events – was being marked by the erection of the altars at Maryport.

It is normally presumed that the altars were dedicated on 3 January, which is the only unchanging date of the three as emperors came and went and so therefore did the date of their accession and birthday. The appropriate sacrifice to Jupiter on that day would have been an ox (Figure 58).

The 17 or 18 altars dedicated to Jupiter by the commanding officers of the First Cohort of Spaniards plus that of Cornelius Peregrinus who we may presume as a tribune was a commander of that regiment, would cover the whole reign of Hadrian from his visit in 122, and presumably the building of the fort then or shortly afterwards, until the death of the emperor in 138. There are, however, three snags. We have just considered the first, that is, whether they only marked one event commemorated in this way, and concluded that it seems likely that each altar was dedicated on 3 January. The second relates to the nature of the

Figure 58. A sacrificial scene on the Bridgeness distance slab on the Antonine Wall showing an ox, sheep and pig waiting to be sacrificed, drawn by Margaret Scott

dedication and the third to the additional information on some of the altars. Should we assume that the altars which were dedicated to more gods than just Jupiter, for example, to the deity of the emperor (Figure 59), were also erected on that date? Could it be that such an altar was erected on one of the emperor's own special days?

The final question relates to the additional information on some altars. Those of Maenius Agrippa, Caballius Priscus, Helstrius Novellus, and two of those of Cammius Maximus are relatively simple dedications, but another of Maximus and those of Censorius Cornelianus and Antistius Lupus Verianus offer more information, as we have seen. In the case of Cammius Maximus, there is an additional appointment squeezed in at the bottom of the inscription, carrying the implication that he is recording a new appointment; on that basis, should we conclude that this is a normal annual Jupiter dedication or a special dedication to the chief god of Rome to thank him for his promotion? Censorinus

Figure 59. On this occasion, Maenius Agrippa dedicated his altar to Jupiter and the Deity of the Emperor (*RIB* 824)

Cornelianus, in a more measured way, also mentions his new posting, but again we may ask, what was the status of his altar? Antistius Lupus Verianus provides a lot of information about himself, including his filiation, voting tribe and origin: he may simply be boasting about his pedigree (the Pooh-Bah of Maryport); by way of comparison, Helstrius Novellus did not even give his praenomen, his first name. The altar of Verianus is also highly decorated, as is that of Cammius Maximus, and in a different way so is that of Censorinus Cornelianus, who also provides additional information about his name and origin: is this relevant? Does the decoration, so much more detailed than the normal Jupiter altars, indicate that these were erected on other occasions?

In summary, we can easily isolate the annual dedications to Jupiter, presumably on 3 January, by Maenius Agrippa, Caballius Priscus, Helstrius Novellus and Cammius Maximus, but the third altar of Maximus and those of Censorius Cornelianus and Antistius Lupus Verianus may be commemorating a different occasion(s).

To return to the letters between Pliny and Trajan; these are interesting because they state that soldiers and provincials would have made the vows together, so a large space would have been required. The excavations of Ian Haynes and Tony Wilmott led to the discovery of a large open space between the classical-style temple at Maryport and the pits where the altars were found in 1870. This seems a likely location for the ceremony. Of course, we do not know if the whole regiment assembled on that day. Some soldiers were probably absent on patrol, collecting supplies or on outpost duties; others, inevitably, were ill in hospital – in a report dating to about 100 on the strength of the regiment based at Vindolanda, 31 soldiers were unfit for service, 15 being sick, 6 wounded and 10 suffering from inflammation of the eyes.

The next questions are, did the altars stand in the open or under cover and how long did they remain there? We know from archaeological discoveries at Osterburken in Germany and Sirmium in Serbia that altars, dedicated by soldiers, were arranged in rows, some still standing on their bases when discovered (Figure 60). These sites provide possible parallels for the situation at Maryport. In 1995 Peter Hill examined the altars and in particular the weathering on their faces and sides, comparing them to the weathering on buildings made from the same stone used to build modern Maryport. He noted that some weathering may have taken place when the altars came into the possession of the Senhouse family and were displayed in their gardens. His wider conclusions, however, were that there was some weathering on the face, the mouldings, the tops and, to a varying extent, on the sides of the altars found in 1870. They were, however, comparatively unweathered when compared to the altars which remained on the surface to be found by later antiquarians but 'they are by no means pristine

Figure 60. The altars found in the shrine at Osterburken on display in the museum in the arrangement that they were found. Photograph the author

and fresh from the hands of the mason, as they would have been if exposed for only one year'; Hill was reacting to the suggestion that each altar had been buried at the end of the year as another was dedicated. Hill, however, concluded that they had been buried relatively early in their lives, perhaps between 20 and 100 years after their dedication; the altars at Sirmium are known to have stood for up to 70 years. Hill pointed out that one altar, that dedicated by Helstrius Novellus, served as a whetstone which shows that it was not carefully buried a year after its erection, nor treated with respect.

It seems possible that as the altars were used as packing blocks in the pits they were still standing in the sacred area when a new use was found for them. This receives some support from the fort at Birdoswald towards the north-east corner of Cumbria. Here many of the 3rd century altars to Jupiter were re-used in the medieval priory at Lanercost and other post-Roman structures. As Mike Jarrett observed, this suggests that they were left standing when the Romans abandoned the fort rather than being buried at an earlier date(s).

A Roman temple

In 1880, Joseph Robinson discovered a stone building at Maryport (Figure 61). It faced north-east and consisted of a rectangular structure 46 ft (14m) long, the main building being 37 ft 9 in (11.5m) long, with a square recess projecting at the west end, by 25 ft (7.6m). At the east end, a wall divided off a small area. The

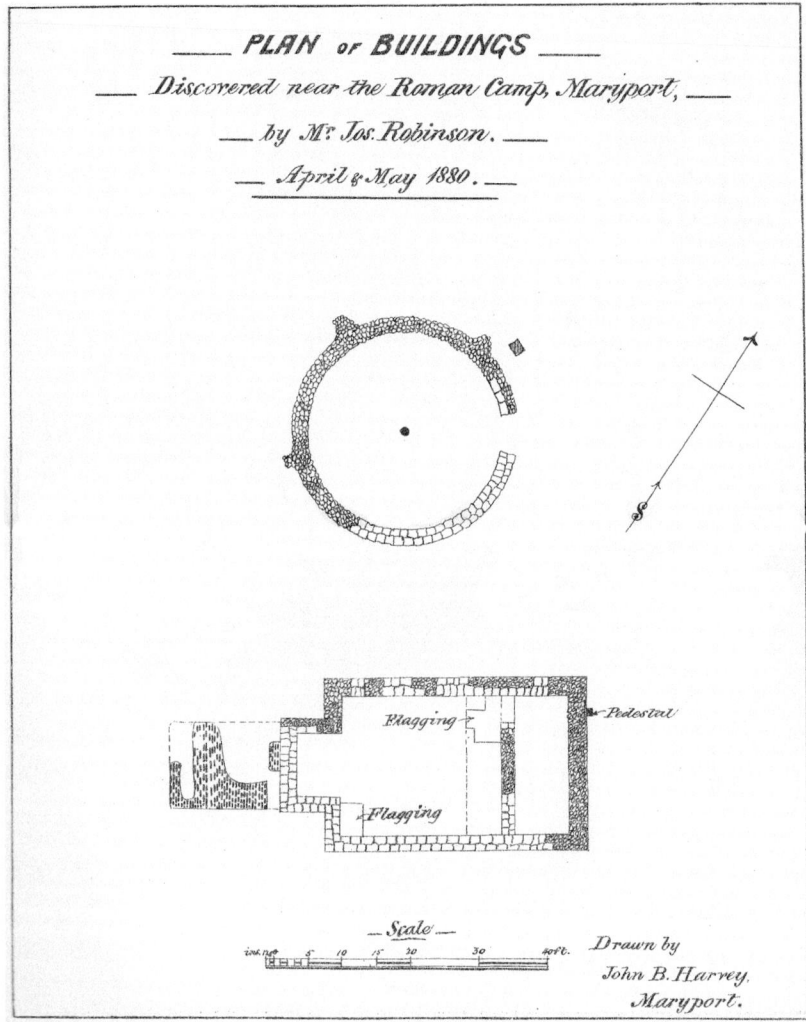

Figure 61. The plan of the temple and circular building excavated by Joseph Robinson

foundations were of clay and cobbles with the wall on top varying in thickness from 2 ft 3 in to 2 ft 9 in (686 to 838mm); no more than two courses of the wall survived. The interior had been flagged, though only two areas of flagging remained, a total of 15 stones being in their original positions. An altar base remained at the northwest corner, that is, we presume, at the rear of the building and to the right of the recess. Its surface was much scored by the plough. Outside the west end of the recess was an area of stones. It was appreciated by Robinson that this was the outer face of the outer wall of the recess which had fallen outwards and had

Figure 62. The temple following excavation by Ian Haynes and Tony Wilmott

somehow survived the ploughing. This indicated that the building had been 18 ft (4.88m) high. Robinson identified the building as a temple.

The building was filled in but then reopened with deleterious effect as the local people came to help themselves to souvenirs. Thus, when Ian Haynes and Tony Wilmott came to re-excavate the building in 2013, they found it significantly more damaged that when last photographed in 1885 (Figure 62). They were able to correct Robinson's measurements to 13.9 by 7.9m. The new excavation allowed a more nuanced interpretation of the building. The small room at the north-east end was a porch. The end foundation did not support a wall but columns.

The team recognised Robinson's temple as something rather more exciting, a classical-style temple. Its location is interesting, lying outside the extra-mural settlement, and it is also noteworthy that it faces towards the highest point of the whaleback ridge where the altars had been reused as packing stones for a timber structure (Figure 63).

Twenty feet (6m) to the seaward side of the temple, Robinson found a round building. Its outside diameter was 34 ft (10.36m) and its wall 2ft 6 in to 2 ft 9 in (762-838mm) wide. In the centre of the building were some stones with, at their centre, an opening about a foot (300m) square. 'The depth of the stones, which

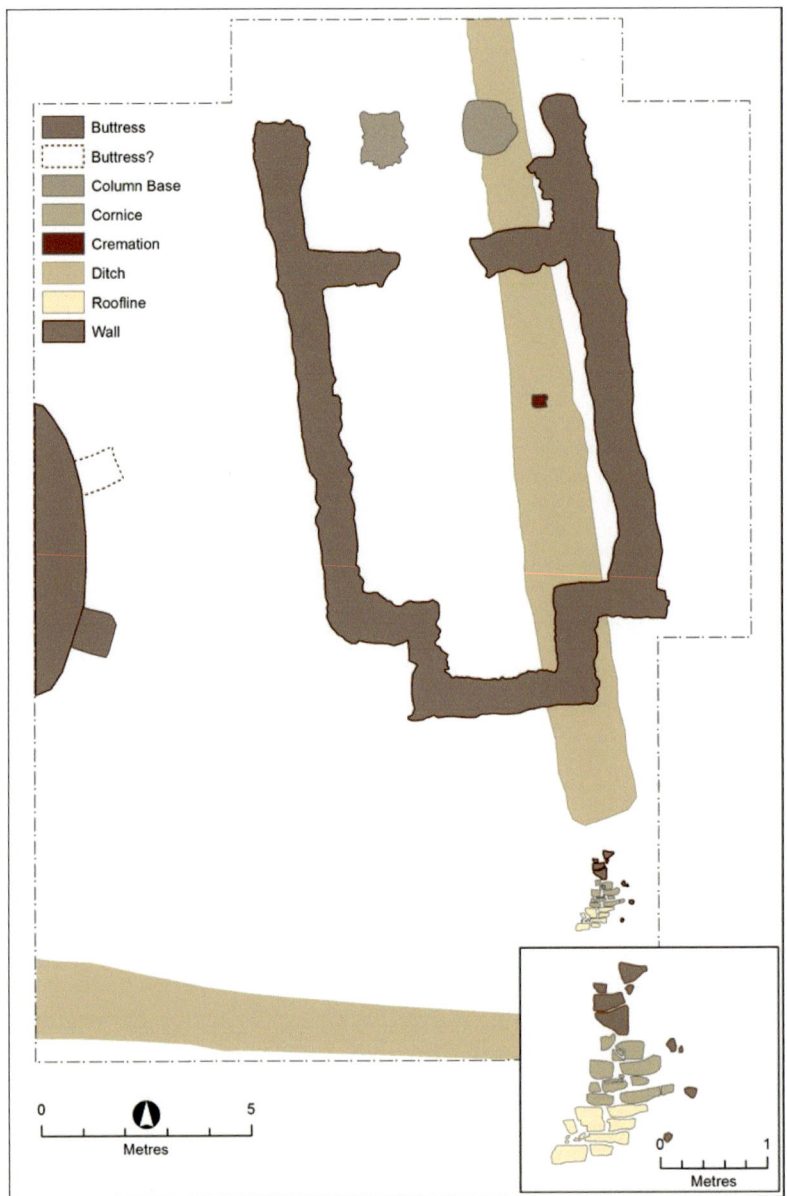

Figure 63. The plan of the temple excavated by Ian Haynes and Tony Wilmott

are rough and unhewn, is three feet [910mm], and, except around the opening, they appear to have been put in without order'. The stones in the centre were interpreted as the base for a support for the roof. On the outside of the wall were four slight projections, each about 18 in (467mm) square, which were interpreted as buttresses. The building was likened to Arthur's O'on near the Antonine Wall, which appears to have been a monument commemorating the Roman victory of 142 which led to the building of the Antonine Wall.

Ian Haynes and Tony Wilmott re-investigated the circular building in 2014. They located its entrance to the north and its timber porch. As yet, the purpose of this circular building cannot be determined. In front of the circular building was a 2m square base formed of several layers of cobbles bound with clay 900mm deep. It may have served as the base for a monument.

The area in front of the temple and the circular building was level and open. Enough cobbling survived subsided into ditches to indicate that the whole area had previously been treated in that way. It was estimated that the open area measured 50m by at least 95m, being bounded by ditches to the north, west and south. On the west side the foundations of part of a building survived, tentatively interpreted as an entrance. This structure had fallen out of use by the late 4th century because it was cut by a ditch containing pottery of that date.

This open space would have been an appropriate location for the ceremonies which took place on 3 January and on the birthday and accession day of the emperor. Here, presumably stood the altars dedicated to Jupiter. The dedication plaque to *Jupiter Optimus Maximus Capitolinus*, it might be expected, had been placed on this temple, but we must await publication of the excavation before it can be seen whether the date of the temple matches the date of the inscription (Figure 64).

Figure 64. The plaque recording a dedication to *Iupiter Optimus Maximus Capitolinus*, and the woodcut prepared for J. C. Bruce, *Lapidarium Septentrionale*, 888, which shows the plaque complete (RIB 832)

The gods of Maryport

We have already seen that the two main gods of the Roman pantheon, Jupiter and Juno, are represented at Maryport. The bearded head of a man, or god, it has been suggested by Jon Coulston, may be Jupiter, but Neptune cannot be ruled out (Figure 65). Several other gods of Rome make brief appearances. Unsurprisingly, Military Mars was the recipient of a dedication, in fact two, by commanders of the First Cohort of the Baetasians (Figure 66).

Neptune received a solitary dedication on a barely legible altar (Figure 67). This was found at the bottom of the cliff when extending the Gas Works below in 1861. The altar may therefore have fallen from the cliff top which would have been an appropriate place for a shrine to the god of the sea. Volcanus or Vulcan also received a single dedication, but he also appears on a broken and unfinished

Figure 65. This is probably the head of a deity. Jupiter has been suggested, but so has Neptune, which would be appropriate for a coastal fort

Figure 66. A dedication to Military Mars by T. Attius Tutor, prefect of the First Cohort of Baetasians (*RIB* 837)

Religion at Maryport

Figure 67. A dedication to Neptune (*RIB* 839)

Figure 68. A dedication to Volcanus/Vulcan by Helstrius Novellus, prefect of the First Cohort of Spaniards (*RIB* 846)

statue (Figures 68 and 69). One commanding officer hedged his bets by dedicating an altar simply to 'the gods and goddesses'. Yet on the sides of his altar are depictions of Mars, bearing a spear and shield, and Hercules, holding his club and the Apples of the Hesperides, and wearing a lion-skin (Figure 70). Hercules also appears on the keystone of an arch, as Jon Coulston states, a fitting position for the strongest of the gods. There is no altar to Minerva, but she appears on an item of sculpture. She holds a spear and a shield and wears a high-girt tunic (Figures 71). The figure beside the representation of a gate has been interpreted as Venus (Figure 72). Mercury may be represented on a damaged stone (Figure 73).

Figure 69. A statue of Vulcan, possibly unfinished

Figure 71. The goddess Minerva holding a spear and shield

Figure 70. Hercules on the side of an altar

Figure 72. A sculptural depiction of a gate with a lady, presumed to be Venus, standing to one side; see Figure 18

RELIGION AT MARYPORT 69

Figure 73. This damaged head may represent Mercury

The largest altar at Maryport is dedicated to the genius of the place, to Eternal Rome, to Good Fate ... and to Fortune the Home-bringer; here was a man pining for his home land and hoping for a safe return, which is not surprising as he came from North Africa (Figures 3 and 33). This enormous stone was found before 1599 in the north corner of the fort. It has been regarded as unusual to find a shrine immediately inside the rampart of the fort, but one such building was found at Vindolanda on Hadrian's Wall in 2009. Cornelius Peregrinus was not the only officer to dedicate to Eternal Rome and to Fortune the Home-bringer, though the second stone does not record a name (Figure 74).

Victory appears in the form of the Emperor's Victory, on two stones of the First Cohort of the Baetasians, who are generally more adventurous

Figure 74. A dedication to Eternal Rome and Fortune the Home-Bringer (*RIB* 840)

in their dedications than the First Cohort of Spaniards (Figure 75). Two winged Victories hold a laurel wreath below an inscription recording the Victory of the Emperors, although, unfortunately, which pair of emperors is not known (Figure 76; see 4 above). This stone was seen by William Camden at Maryport in 1599 (Figure 4). Hermione, who we have already met, dedicated an altar to the Valour of the Emperor (Figure 77).

Gods are sometimes represented by three identical figures which serves to emphasise their powers. A damaged stone from Maryport is such a depiction. Two of the three female figures survive; more of the 'lost' figure used to survive, but since its discovery, and its record in 1875, the head and part of the upper half of the body have broken off (Figures 78 and 79). Unusually, the figures are naked, and the fact that they are females is highlighted by the emphasis on their genitalia. Jon Coulston notes that Mother Goddesses are

Figure 75. T. Attius Tutor dedicated this altar to the Emperor's Victory (*RIB* 842)

Figure 76. The Victory of the Emperors (*RIB* 844); this inscription was recorded as being at Netherhall in 1599; see Figure 4

Religion at Maryport

Figure 77. The dedication to the Valour of the Emperor by Hermione (*RIB* 845)

Figure 78. A triad of ?Sea Nymphs

Figure 79. A woodcut showing the triad before part of the stone was lost, reproduced from J. C. Bruce, *Lapidarium Septentrionale*, 896

Figure 80. A goddess sitting on a chair holding a possible cornucopia

not depicted naked and he suggests that the figures are Nymphs, possibly Sea Nymphs.

Another female figure is crudely represented, sitting on a chair (Figure 80). As she is holding what appears to be a cornucopia in her right hand, she is probably Fortuna. A sculpture of a genius – the god or spirit of the place – shows him holding a cornucopia and a *patera*, that is a metal pan (Figure 81).

Maryport had international links through its officers and at least two other men, but foreign gods hardly appear. There is a single representation of an oriental god, Sol (Figure 82). He was carved on a key-stone. Around his head are thirteen rays; he wears a cloak and in one hand holds an orb while the other is raised in order to hold another object, perhaps a spear.

Local gods are little represented on inscriptions; Labareus, a German, dedicated his altar to Setlocenia, who is otherwise unknown, and Julius Civilis to Belatucadrus, who was probably the main god of the self-governing state of the Carvetii based in the Eden Valley, as we have seen. But local gods appear

Figure 81. The statuette of a Genius – the god or spirit of the place – holding a cornucopia and *patera*, that is, a metal pan

Figure 82. The god Sol on the keystone of an arch

magnificently in a handful of items of sculpture, in particular the horned gods. There are several representations of this in northern England, so many that Anne Ross called him the horned god of the Brigantes, the tribe which occupied most of that area.

The carvings are certainly crude, and not all the gods have horns (Figures 83 and 84). They have a certain feeling of vitality. Anne Ross suggested that the feet of the horned god, turning left or right, give an impression of movement. The god carries weapons, a rectangular shield in one instance, a round one in another, and a spear. He is naked, and with his penis clearly visible. The god therefore appears to have two attributes, one military and the other relating to fertility.

There are several other phallic stones at Maryport, including the Serpent Stone to be discussed below under burial. There is an incised phallus facing what may

Figure 83. A horned god holding a spear and a rectangular shield

Figure 84. The depiction of a Celtic god, though without horns, holding a spear and a round shield

Figure 85. The phallus of Marcus Septimius

Figure 86. A phallic stone

Figure 87. A phallic stone

be a vulva or the evil eye, warding off the evil eye being the special purpose of the phallus (Figure 85). The inscription beside the phallus reads, the phallus of Marcus Septimius. The phallus on two other stones is shown in relief (Figures 86 and 87).

RELIGION AT MARYPORT 75

Figure 88. The goddess Epona

Another Celtic god was Epona, the horse-goddess and the patroness of soldiers who worked with horses and pack animals, a very appropriate deity to appear at a cavalry fort (Figure 88). She is rarely depicted in Britain, but her name may be related to the tribe, the Epidii, which lived in the Kintyre peninsula in modern Argyll. Setlocenia is represented by a relief. She is identified by the vessel which she holds in her right hand. Her name means the goddess of long life.

Celtic motifs in the form of the wheel appear on the altars of the First Cohort of Spaniards (Figures 31, 37 and 38). As Miranda Green notes, the appearance of a Celtic symbol on the otherwise classical military monuments is curious. The wheel, however, is but one of several different motifs which appear on the altars of this regiment. Dot-and-circle and concentric circles seem to be characteristic of the altars of Maenius Agrippa, and also appear on two of the altars of Caballius Priscus (Figures 30 and 59). Both these men held the rank of tribune and therefore served successively at Maryport. A circle appears on the altar of Helstrius Novellus (Figure 32). Other ornaments are demi-lunes, triangles and zig-zags, but these do not appear to have a religious significance, at least not one that has been yet recognised (Figures 28, 37, 38 and 39). They do, however,

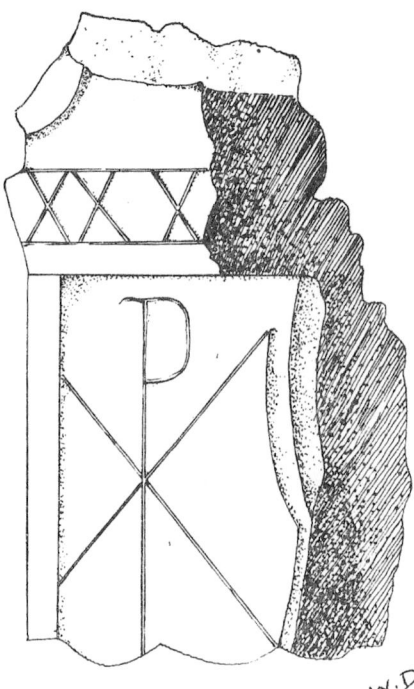

Figure 89. A Chi-Rho symbol on a stone now lost. Published without comment in W. Hutchinson, *The History of the County of Cumberland*, Carlisle, 1794, vol. 2, pl. v, no. 39; this drawing prepared by Wilfrid Dodds for Mike Jarrett in 1954.

pull the altars together as a group and demonstrate, as Mike Jarrett pointed out, 'a highly individual style of ornament, elements of which may be paralleled elsewhere though the style itself seems to be unique to Maryport'.

We may also note that the appearance of similar details on different altars have allowed Mike Jarrett to suggest that the altars dedicated by Attius Tutor, and also probably Ulpius Titianus, were the work of the same craftsman, presumably a soldier, who produced altars of higher than normal standard. If it was the same letter-cutter, Peter Hill has suggested that his improvement in skills demonstrates that Titianus held his command before Tutor.

Finally, amongst all these gods of Rome and Britain, a lost and fragmentary stone bears the Christian symbol known as the Chi-Rho (Figure 89). These are two Greek letters, X standing for C and the P (pronounced R in Greek), the first two letters of Christ.

As already noted, the relationship between the dedicator and the god was personal, the god's support being sought for a particular action. We have also seen that there were official religious occasions. A document dating to the third century and found at Dura on the eastern frontier is a list of religious ceremonies. As these involve sacrifices to Jupiter, Juno, Minerva, Mars – the gods of the Roman pantheon – for events relating to the emperor and his predecessors over the previous 200 years, there is a strong reason to view the document as a list of *official* religious ceremonies. There are 41 ceremonies listed for nine months, so there were perhaps 54 in the whole year. But we do not know the form of the ceremony. Was it a short simple ceremony performed by the commanding officer (Figure 58)? Did the whole regiment parade? Were the soldiers given a day off? These are questions we cannot answer.

Death and burial

Roman law forbad burial within built-up areas. Cemeteries were therefore out of town and tended to be placed beside the roads leading out of the urban area. At Maryport, the presence of tombstones and burials indicate the location of cemeteries. There is also an indication that an area for burial was specifically designated on a tombstone found in 1966 re-used as a paving stone in a building dating to the fourth century in the north-east corner of the fort. The stone was erected by Julius Senecianus to his most dutiful wife Sotera, 'as the place allowed'. This phrase is not attested elsewhere and its interpretation is nor certain. Here, it is likely to mean that the body was buried in the designated area, that is, the official cemetery.

Figure 90. The fir cone

In 1880, Joseph Robinson found several burials to the north-east of the fort. Around a pavement measuring 13 by 6 ft (4 by 1.8m) he 'found burials, the remains of funeral pyres, and calcined bones, ... [and] numerous urns', while under the pavement were four burials. A little to the east were three cists. Here, also, Robinson found the Serpent Stone, two fragments of a second stone bearing a serpent and a stone fir cone, a symbol often associated with death (Figure 90). Nearby, in a hedge, was recovered the tombstone of a child; another tombstone had been previously found in this area. This cemetery lay immediately beyond the north-eastern edge of the extra-mural settlement. A fragmentary tombstone was found even further north in the early 1950s. The stone may have been carried to this spot, 1.5 km (a mile) north-east of the fort, in order to re-use it in a later building.

In 1880, Robinson also found a large number of burials beside the circular building. A funeral pyre lay to one side of the building with a layer of charcoal 14 in (356mm) thick. Other burials lay to the north. This cemetery also lay beyond the extra-mural settlement, in this case on its eastern side.

Figure 91. Two burials in the cemetery excavated by CFA Archaeology Ltd. To the left are the burial vessels with their contents; to the right after emptying

Another cemetery was discovered to the east of the fort in 2010 by CFA Archaeology Ltd (Figure 91). The cemetery lay on the south side of the road leading towards Papcastle, the Roman fort at Cockermouth. On a low knoll were found ten cremations and the base of a marker stone, presumably indicating the site of another burial. One pit was excavated. Two pots lay within, both grey ware jars, one containing cremated bones together with some charred hazelnut shells and grape pips. As the edge of the pit could not be determined, it was presumed that it was backfilled immediately after use. Iron objects in the pits included nails and hob-nails from foot wear, so presumably the dead were cremated with their boots on. The cremated bones indicate that one body was of an adult, and another possible a juvenile.

We have seen that tombstones are indicators of the location of cemeteries. The tombstone of Rianorix was found south-east of the fort, beside the place where the Roman road leading east to Papcastle crossed the River Ellen (Figure 92). This would be an appropriate place for a cemetery. Rianorix is presumed to have been male, but Tancorix, whose name has the same ending, buried beside the nearby fort at Old Carlisle, was female.

Excavations by Ian Haynes and Tony Wilmott in 2011 and 2012 led to the discovery of yet another cemetery at Maryport (Figure 93). This lay on the summit of the hill north of the site, and immediately north of the 1870s pits. Seven graves of stone-lined long-cists were excavated. The earlier three were aligned north-south, but the later four were orientated east-west, which might suggest a Christian association. One of the earlier graves produced a radiocarbon date of 240-340 and another a coin of the 360s or 370s. Few bones survived, but it would appear that at least one of the bodies was that of a child.

Figure 92. The stone recording Rianorix

Figure 93. The cemetery north of the 1870 altar find spot excavated by Ian Haynes and Tony Wilmott

Figure 94. The Serpent Stone as it is today

Figure 95. The Serpent Stone as found

So, we appear to have several cemeteries at Maryport. One lay to the north of the fort, beside the road leading northwards along the coast; a second beside the circular building, the other three were to the east, two located beside roads.

The most celebrated discovery in a cemetery at Maryport was the Serpent Stone (Figure 94). The stone stands 1.296m high. It consists of three parts, a base 432mm high, a tapering shaft 559mm tall and a head 305mm high. At the top is an iron peg set in lead; we do not know the reason for this. On one side of the stone is a serpent and on the other is a human face with two serpents above and two fishes below; unfortunately the serpents have broken off since the discovery and the fishes are scarcely legible (Figure 95). The face has lentoid eyes and a triangular nose above a moustache. Realistically, lines run down to the corners of the mouth, which is slightly open. Beneath the chin is a torque, a sort of necklace (Figure 96).

This remarkable carving had probably started out life as a large altar. This was cut down to create the large phallus, which is the stone today. Giant phallic

Figure 96. The face on the Serpent Stone

Figure 97. One of the heads found at Burrow Heights near Lancaster. Photograph the author

objects were used in Greek and Roman ceremonies such as fertility rites. The excavators drew attention to the large phallus containing a serpent at the tumulus of Alyattes at Sardis in western Turkey. The head at the top of the stone may relate to the Celtic cult of the head, and this might be supported by the torque round the neck. Sometimes heads appear in funerary contexts, such as those at Burrow Heights south of Lancaster (Figure 97). Snakes are connected both with Celtic gods and in Roman contexts where they act in a friendly manner protecting people from the evil eye. The Serpent Stone therefore appears to combine both Celtic and Roman elements as well as funerary and living aspects.

The second serpent stone was wider, with a base of similar height to the first stone. It had a hole in it, possible to receive a column.

Figure 98. The tombstone of a cavalryman

One of the frequent problems at Maryport is that we do not known the find spots of most of the objects. This is the case with one military tombstone, that of a cavalryman (Figure 98). Unfortunately, this is badly eroded, but the main features are clear. The rider sits on his horse, smaller than in real life so as to fit into the available space. The horse is stepping over rough ground. The rider holds the reins, and his calf and foot are outlined. He appears to have a cloak, in the words of Jon Coulston, billowing out behind him. Importantly, there is no prostrate enemy below the horse's hoofs and there is no indication that the rider wore armour. This suggests a date in the second or third centuries for the tombstone as the earlier style was to show the soldier in armour and his enemy at his feet.

The tombstone of this cavalryman is very weathered; a second possible tombstone of a soldier appears to have been smashed (Figure 99). The head of the figure is now lost, but his clothing remains. He wears a cloak and one or two tunics, one appearing to fall down well below his knee. In his left-hand he holds a square box; this may be a box of writing tablets, an item which appears on the tombstones of some soldiers. An alternative interpretation is that the object is a jewellery box, and therefore the person is female. There is another item below the box, but its nature cannot be determined.

Figure 99. The damaged tombstone which probably depicts a soldier

Chapter 5

Maryport in its setting

Seated it was upon the height of a hill　　　　　　　　　　　William Camden

A Roman fort sat in a landscape which it had inherited and then influenced. The Romans chose to place their fort in an advantageous position, on a low hill overlooking the estuary of a small river (Figure 100). It is noteworthy that they did not place their fort on top of the hill, but on its seaward side, perhaps where it would be a little sheltered, and certainly where it would have had wide views.

Figure 100. The cliffs of Maryport today looking towards the museum

It is too easy to seek to impress our views on the past. For the Romans, the top of the hill is not where they wanted their fort to be placed. Nor was it where other people wanted to live. In fact, it does not appear to have been built on during the Roman period; Ian Haynes and Tony Wilmott found no buildings there, only ditches and a possibly floor surface. It was only at the very end of Roman Britain, or even a little later, that a timber structure was erected on the top of the hill. This was formed of posts each about 300mm square, but the function of the building is not yet understood. One pointer to the date is that the ditch of a circular enclosure on top of the hill appears to have been open at roughly the same time that the pits were dug for the fragment of an altar was found in it as well as late fourth century pottery.

The fort was linked to the road network of military deployment by roads (Figure 101). One led to the north-east, linking Maryport to the forts at Beckfoot and

Figure 101. The pattern of military deployment in northern England. Copyright the author

Figure 102. The hollow crossing the field diagonally is believed to mark the route of the Roman road approaching the fort from Papcastle. Photograph the author

Bowness-on-Solway. The road to the south led to Moresby, whose earthworks are still visible today. The third road led inland to the fort at Papcastle, just outside modern Cockermouth (Figure 102). Papcastle was linked to Carlisle by a road which ran inland and parallel to the coast and was probably earlier than the coastal route. For speed of travel, the quickest route from Maryport to Carlisle was probably via Papcastle.

Rural settlements

Farming had begun on the Solway Plain before 3000 BC. At first, lighter soils were tilled and trees were felled. By the centuries immediately before the arrival of the Romans, the tree cover had been reduced to about what it is today. There was some cereal cultivation, but as the west coast received heavy rainfall, pasture was more important than in the lands east of the Pennines.

Aerial survey has revealed farmsteads usually dated to the late prehistoric and Roman periods on the Solway Plain. Few have been excavated, but some conclusions are possible. Barri Jones has noted that the sites on the Solway plain tend to be oval in shape with normally only one ditch, compared to settlements north of the estuary which usually had two or more ditches. Jones suggested that the protection provided by Hadrian's Wall allowed the southern sites to be less heavily defended.

One of the sites revealed through geopohysical survey at Maryport was a rectilinear settlement in the field generally known as the Deer Park Field south-east of the fort, and surprisingly close to the urban conglomeration of fort and extra-mural settlement (Figure 48). On a hillock sat a rectilinear enclosure of the type well-known in northern Britain as a farmstead of the Iron Age or Roman British period. It even appeared to contain a round hut. Its entrance lay to the north-east (away from the prevailing south-westerly wind) and a branch from the Roman road leading to the east gate of the fort pointed in the direction of this entrance. Excavation by CFA Archaeology Ltd has revealed further details (Figures 103, 104 and 105). Perhaps most interesting, the settlement revealed through geophysical survey was not the earliest enclosure on the site. It was preceded by a circular enclosure almost the same size as its successor and defined by a ditch up to just over 1m wide and 620mm deep. Debris from the later farmstead included domestic items such as pottery sherds, glass and small fragments of worked metal, while slag pointed to industrial activity at the site. Fired clay probably derived from the building.

This excavation revealed information about one of the most import aspects of life at Maryport, food. The fill of a ditch included grains of wheat and barley, together with a high concentration of free-threshing wheat spikelet forks and glume bases probably from spelt wheat. Hazelnut shells and grape pips were found in one of the jars used to hold cremated bones.

Maryport lies at the south-west corner of the Solway Plain, where the Lake District hills approach the sea, and where the modern town of Workington has obscured and removed traces of earlier occupation. Yet, two other Iron Age settlements are known in its vicinity, both examined by Bob Bewley. One lies to the south, at Ewanrigg (Figure 106). This was a defended settlement with its origins probably in the Bronze Age and continuing in occupation until the late fourth century AD. The farmstead was surrounded by two ditches. Within the enclosure a paved area was investigated. Below this was a pit, probably of Roman date, containing carbonised grain. This was not well preserved but appeared to include barley and spelt wheat. The pit may have been used for the storage of grain and was possibly lined with straw. Elsewhere, emmer wheat was recorded.

The longevity of settlement at this location is shown by the existence of a Bronze Age cemetery only 60m to the south. Here 28 burials were recorded, of which 26 were cremations and two inhumations. It was possible to identify six female burials and five males. Within the cremations were toggles and pins made of bone. Radiocarbon dating points to occupation between about 2500 and 1500 BC.

To the north of Maryport lies another whaleback hill, Swarthy Hill (Figure 107). On its northern flank sits a Roman tower and on its southern the milefortlet 21.

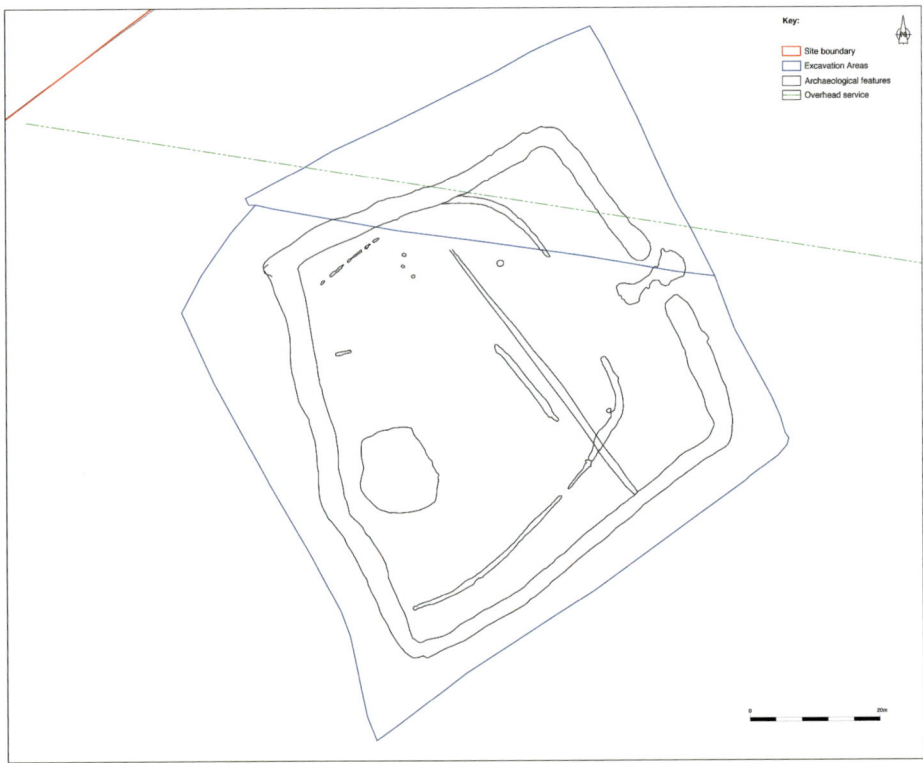

Figure 103. The plan of the rural settlement excavated by CFA Archaeology Ltd; for the geophysical plan of the site see Figure 48 where the settlement is at the bottom of the plan

But on the top of the hill is a settlement defenced by three ditches. Excavation in 1988 by Bob Bewley, who also examined Ewanrigg, produced a radiocarbon date of 450 +/- 50 BC, but the difficulties of tying down radiocarbon dates in the Iron Age results in a wider range of potential dates. Nevertheless, this is sufficient to determine occupation of the site in the Iron Age.

We can now see that in the area of Maryport were three rural settlements, all probably occupied at the same time as the Roman fort, though with long antecedents. Further, we know something of the food consumed at them. In spite of the amount of pasture, two of the three sites have produced evidence for the consumption of cereals, namely barley, emmer and spelt wheat. The hazel nuts found at the rural settlement in Maryport were probably gathered locally. The grapes, however, were an exotic import and are likely to have found their way to the farm through the shops in the civil settlement on the other side of the hill.

Figure 104. Composite aerial view, created by Merlin UAS Ltd, of the excavation of the rural settlement by CFA Archaeology Ltd; the ditch is defined by the narrow cuts across it

Figure 105. A section across the ditch of the rural settlement excavated by CFA Archaeology Ltd

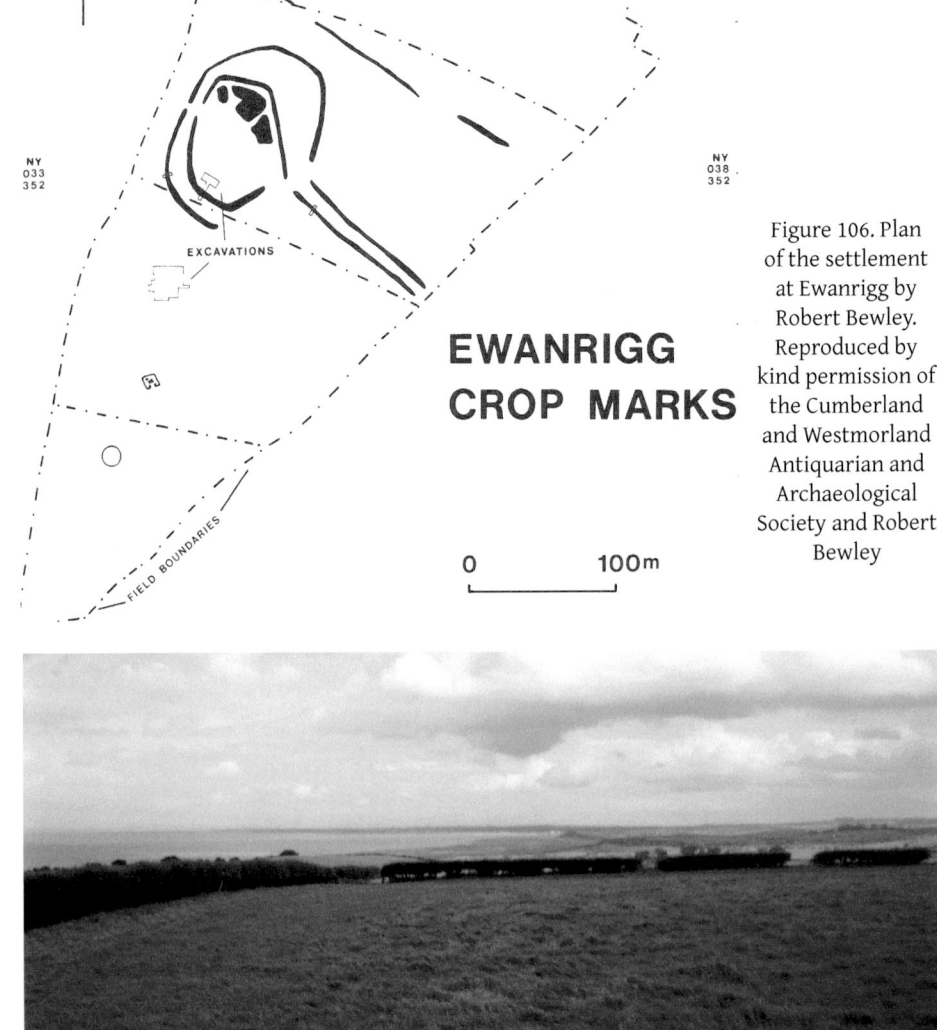

Figure 106. Plan of the settlement at Ewanrigg by Robert Bewley. Reproduced by kind permission of the Cumberland and Westmorland Antiquarian and Archaeological Society and Robert Bewley

Figure 107. Swarthy Hill as viewed from the fort at Maryport: the dark triangle beside the coast to the right of centre in the photograph is the hill. Photograph the author

It is difficult to say more about the relationship between town and country at Maryport. If we look further afield, however, we may note the discussion of Old Carlisle by Barri Jones. Here the earthworks of the fort survive beside the road leading from Papcastle to Carlisle. Aerial survey has revealed traces of strip houses outside the fortfort, passing from this extra-mural settlement into the countryside are tracks leading to fields. Many of these fields are less than one acre in size (0.4 ha) and as such might be better classed as horticultural plots or allotments. As at Maryport, a Roman road or track links the Roman settlement to a rural farmstead.

It is, as yet, difficult to go further than that. Only archaeological excavation can demonstrate close links between the fort and its surrounding settlement, that is, the town, and the countryside in which it sits. Even then, we have a problem. Several surveys have demonstrated that Roman artefacts drop in quantity the further from the town, even in the more civilised southern part of the province. In northern Britain, the problem for many years has been the lack of Roman artefacts from the rural settlements of the indigenous populations, and without such evidence it is difficult to offer conclusions about the relationships between town and country. It might be expected that the army would seek supplies from the local people, and indeed most Roman forts in Cumbria were situated in good farming land. It might also be expected that the rural farmsteads would supply some recruits for the Roman army, but if they did the soldiers did not send Roman knick-knacks home to their mums.

Chapter 6

Life on the edge of empire

The eyes of the legion   Inscription on a rock at Nineveh

So how did the 500 soldiers based at Maryport spend their time? Perhaps the first question to ask is, were there 500 soldiers at the fort? There are incredibly few surviving documents which provide information on the strength of the Roman army. The figures quoted in this book – units of 500 or 1000, infantry or cavalry or mixed – are themselves approximations. The small unit, called *quingenaria*, that is 500, actually contained either 480, 512 or 608 soldiers. The unit entitled *milliaria* was either 768, 800 or 1050 strong.

But even then, these figures are theoretical. A small number of documents exist which show that units were below strength, in one case by as much as 25%. When we examine the plans of forts, we can also see that sometimes not enough barracks were provided for the unit based there. At Birrens, just across the Solway from Maryport – and with its earthworks still visible – the fort appears to have been planned with the understanding that some of its soldiers would always be outposted. These outposts were the fortlets of south-west Scotland (Figure 108).

Can we say what happened at Maryport? The short answer is that we cannot. What we can do is to look at what happened elsewhere in Britain, and elsewhere in the Roman empire.

The main purpose of the Roman army had been to extend the Roman state. The Romans saw it as their mission to conquer the world – rather like white men in the 19th century – and the means to accomplish this was their army. In the last two centuries of the Republic, the empire was extended enormously by arrogant

Figure 108. An artist's impression of the Roman fortlet at Barburgh Mill in south-west Scotland. Drawn by Michael J. Moore

aristocrats such as Pompey and Julius Caesar. The seizure of power by Caesar's heir, Octavian, brought about a step change. Whereas in the previous decades the empire had lurched forward at the behest of the individual generals, now Octavian, re-branded as Augustus, took hold of the situation. Although we have no surviving document setting out his plan, it is possible to suggest what it was by examining his actions.

We can guess that Augustus, having achieved supreme power by 30 BC, set about dealing with the problems he had inherited, tidying up the corners of his empire which his predecessors had thought too troublesome to deal with. In the process, he brought the edge of his empire to the Sahara Desert in the south, the sea in the west, the Rhine and Danube to the north, and the Parthian Empire

Figure 109. Criffel as viewed from the fort at Maryport

to the east. In his testament, he stated that the empire should stay within the boundaries he had set. It didn't quite work out like that as Claudius invaded Britain and Trajan conquered Dacia while other emperors continue to tweak its boundaries, as did Septimius Severus in Britain in 208-11. But, crucially, the trajectory changed. Instead of continuing expansion, emperors became more concerned to protect what they inherited. The army, so long the blood-thirsty agents of expansion, had to find a new role. This role was to defend the empire's frontiers – and to deal with any internal insurrections. Their new role led to the construction of frontiers such as Hadrian's Wall. These frontiers had several functions. They defined the edge of the empire, served as a base for the army to defend the empire, restricted raiding and other low intensity threats and controlled access to the empire.

With that in mind, what did the soldiers based at Maryport do? The units based there sat on the very edge of the empire, facing the hill known today as Criffel across the Solway. No one can stand at Maryport and not appreciate that hill, just across the water, in foreign territory (Figure 109). But were the people of that area hostile? That is more difficult to determine. The Romans certainly liked to control the states immediately beyond their borders, interfering with their politics as necessary. Towards the end of the 2nd century, in the 190s, we are informed that the Romans had treaties with the Caledonians and their neighbours the Maeatae, who probably lived in the Forth Valley around Stirling. In the 360s we are also informed that the peoples living north of Hadrian's Wall broke their treaty relations. So, it is probable that some sort of relationship existed with the people of the Criffel area, even if it was imposed on them, and it is possible that the soldiers of Maryport crossed the Solway to ensure that the agreed arrangements were upheld.

Warfare on the frontier

That may have been the theory, but warfare did break out on the northern frontier of Britain. At the beginning of the reign of the Emperor Hadrian in 117, 'the Britons could not be held under control' (Figure 110). A soldier was buried at Vindolanda about this time, having died in a war. Two generations later, the senator and courtier Cornelius Fronto, remarked that the number of soldiers killed in Britain in Hadrian's reign could be compared to those lost in his Jewish War, the Bar Kokhba uprising, that is, a considerable number. We do not know how long this war lasted, but the earliest date for the striking of the coin to celebrate victory was in 119.

The next emperor, Antoninus Pius, ordered his general to advance north and build a new Wall, the frontier known as the Antonine Wall, across the Forth-Clyde isthmus. The reason for this advance is not clear, but most ancient historians believe that the victory and extension of the empire was in order to provide the new emperor, who had no military experience, with a successful military operation which would underpin his position in Rome; such actions are not unknown today.

Figure 110. A coin of the Emperor Hadrian. Reproduced by kind permission of the Great North Museum and the Society of Antiquaries of Newcastle upon Tyne

At the beginning of the next reign, that is in 161, war was again threatening in Britain and a new governor was dispatched to the province. Shortly after 180, there was a major invasion of the province. A general and the troops that he had with him were killed and it took about two years for order to be restored. Just a dozen years later there was further trouble on the frontier. The governor of Britain took his army to the continent to challenge his rival Septimius Severus ... and lost. The new governor sent out to run the province found himself at a disadvantage on the northern frontier and was compelled to purchase peace, receiving back a few prisoners. By 206, the advantage had turned in favour of the Romans, but Severus decided he would come to Britain to campaign against the Caledonians. He fought his way into north-east Scotland and brought his enemy to peace talks, but they rebelled and, while campaigning was being renewed, Severus died in York in February 211. As a result, his scheme came to an abrupt end. His sons abandoned his conquests and returned to Rome.

For the next century we have very little evidence for anything on the northern frontier, but in 305 the Emperor Constantius I and his son, the later Emperor Constantine, campaigned against the Picts. Constantine's son, Constans, came to Britain in the winter of 342/3; we are not told the reason though it is usually suggested that it was to deal with trouble on the northern frontier. The events of the 360s are clearer, with warfare being recorded in 360, 364 and 367, while in 382 Magnus Maximus conducted a vigorous campaign in which he defeated the Picts and Scots, who had carried out an invasion. Finally, in a statement relating to 400, the Emperor Honorius' chief minister, Stilicho, is recording as taking action against the Picts and the Scots. At about the same time, a field army consisting of six regiments was sent to take up residence in the island, though we do not know where they were based.

What part did the soldiers of Maryport play in these events? Obviously, it is not possible to say as there are no specific statements relating to units based in the fort. The nearest that we can come to involvement in fighting is the award of Roman citizenship to the men of the First Cohort of Baetasians, apparently during the invasion of southern Scotland at the beginning of the reign of Antoninus Pius, and before they took up residence at Maryport. The award of the title *Aelia* to the First Cohort of Spaniards, in this case after they had moved on from Maryport, suggests valorous action in a war. Nevertheless, we can presume that the units of Maryport participated in the wars which occurred in the reign of nearly every emperor in the second century.

Life on the frontier

When not fighting, more mundane actions such as patrolling, supervising treaty arrangements and seeking out bandits were undertaken. The Roman

Figure 111. The milefortlet at Swarthy Hill looking south-west towards the whaleback hill of Maryport. Photograph Andrew Selkirk

Empire was not as peaceful as usually assumed and the Lake District would have offered a haven for bandits. Supply routes needed protecting. Documents from the eastern provinces of the empire demonstrate that soldiers regularly undertook such duties, operating on ships as well as land, and themselves collecting supplies.

An understanding of military deployment can lead to a better appreciation of the concerns of the army. When the fort at Maryport was first occupied, it formed part of a complex system of frontier installations focussed on Hadrian's Wall but extending to its east, south and north as well as west. Hadrian's Wall ended at Bowness-on-Solway. The curtain wall itself might have ended here, but the smaller installations, the milecastles and turrets, continued down the coast to a little further south than Maryport, though here called milefortlets and towers (Figure 111). Their existence points to a concern with a threat from across the estuary. But the rub is that when Hadrian's Wall was reoccupied after 158 on the abandonment of the Antonine Wall, none of the towers along the coast were re-occupied and few of the milefortlets, and even the ones which were re-occupied didn't last long. If there was a serious threat from across the estuary, we might expect that these sites would have been re-commissioned in 158 and retained thereafter.

If there was no threat from across the Solway, why was the fort maintained at Maryport for nearly 300 years when the smaller military installations were abandoned? Partly, the answer, we might expect, was the threat from the north, from the Caledonians and their descendants the Picts living in mainland

Scotland, which required a strong force to remain in the vicinity of the northern frontier.

In the third century, when we know of no warfare on the northern frontier, it would appear that many units were withdrawn from their forts in the north of England in the hinterland of Hadrian's Wall; the evidence lies in the appearance at these forts of new-style units in the fourth century indicating that their predecessors were no longer present.

In the fourth century we can certainly appreciate a reason for a fort being retained at Maryport for now there was a threat from across a different stretch of water, the Irish Sea. The Scots, then resident in Ireland, and the Attacotti, a little-known people but certainly living in Ireland, were mentioned as threats to peace on the frontier – the Scots were described as ranging far and wide and causing great devastation. We know something of the measures taken to protect the western seaboard from these raiders. New forts were built at Cardiff and Lancaster (Figure 112). Smaller stations were placed in north-west Wales,

Figure 112. A gate of the late Roman fort at Cardiff as rebuilt by the 3rd and 4th Marquis of Bute in the years following 1869 (work was not completed until 1927). Photograph the author

with an observation tower on Holyhead Mountain on Anglesey. Maryport would have been an obvious fort to be given extra protection. It would not be surprising therefore if external bastions were added to the fort walls at this time (Figure 113). This, however, is supposition. All that we can say is that there was a Roman presence within the fort, presumably military, up to the end of Roman Britain. And we can add that two of the men who may have served in the last days of the fort were [S]purcio, who lived for 61 years (Figure 114), and Rianorix, whose tombstones have been found outside the fort (Figure 92).

Figure 113. The south-west corner of the fort with the platform which may have been the location of an external bastion visible to the right. Photograph Andrew Selkirk

Figure 114. The tombstone of [S]purcio

Naval duties?

It has often been suggested that the duties of the soldiers based at Maryport included maritime activities of some sort. The reasons vary from the simple – the fort sat on the sea at the estuary of a river and therefore the soldiers 'must have had' a naval role – to the more complex – the title 'tribune' given to the commander of the First Cohort of Spaniards was not because of the type of regiment he commanded but because he had special maritime duties. The size of the strong-room has been cited, and it was larger than normal, but the implications of that are totally uncertain. Perhaps the best reason is that offered by Roger Wilson, namely that navigation of the Solway Estuary to the north was difficult and that Maryport served a special role where supplies were unloaded and transported onwards by barge or by land.

In truth, a naval role cannot be proved. We do know that there was a British Fleet, but it was based in the Channel forts and we have no evidence for it operating on the west coast of Britain. In any case, the role of the fleet was military – it was an offensive and defensive force – not supply. So far as we can tell, many, perhaps most, of the supplies for the army were provided by civilians and transported by civilian merchants.

The fort at Maryport was a normal size. No granaries are known within it which might have been used for the temporary storage of supplies being transported to other forts. The title of the commander – and there were only two tribunes – was based upon the size and status of the unit and not putative special duties. In short, Maryport was a normal fort, one of many in the hinterland of Hadrian's Wall whose primary duties were the protection of the empire.

Training

Fighting may have been intermittent on the northern frontier, and the role of the regiments based at Maryport uncertain, but the soldiers had to be trained to be ready for action. According to Vegetius, writing in the late fourth century, and other Roman writers, recruits should be trained in the use of weapons twice a day, in drill, the digging of ditches, the construction of palisades, running, jumping, swimming, vaulting, felling trees, and route marches four times a month. And similar training should have been maintained throughout their service.

We know of two locations in forts for such training. One was in a large hall in the centre of a fort. Not all forts, however, had such a hall and one is not known at Maryport. The other place was the parade-ground. Little is known of these. They are recorded in ancient literature, at least by implication. The

Emperor Hadrian inspected regiments of the army in Africa in 128 and parts of the inscriptions erected to record these events survive. They record that the soldiers took part in mock combat. Such events – practices for real combat – are also described by one of Hadrian's governor, Arrian in his *Tactitcal Handbook*.

In some instances, flat areas outside Roman forts have been identified as parade grounds; one lies beside the fort at Hardknott. As we have seen, an area beside Pudding Pie Hill was identified as a parade ground in 1891. This, however, might have been a flight of fancy – not least as it had not been recognised before even by the Ordnance Survey – encouraged by an interpretation of the prehistoric burial mound as a Roman military saluting base. The latest review of the evidence has dismissed this proposed parade ground. Yet, that was before the excavations of the Maryport and District Archaeological Society at the beginning of this century. In the area where Father Cummins placed the parade ground, and the Ordnance Survey mapped it, the excavators found a cobbled surface. This trench, though, was within the area suggested in a later season to lie within the early fort and the cobbles therefore could be part of a road or courtyard. In any case, Arrian stated that once the area for the cavalry exercises had been levelled, the ground was turned over to make it soft and springy. A cobbled area, presumably originally gravelled, would have been used for infantry training, not cavalry exercises.

Remarkably, a second parade ground was also identified at Maryport. This was a result of the study of the altars found in 1870 and on other occasions, all dedicated to Jupiter. It was argued that the altars had been erected beside a parade ground. This identification has also suffered from closer inspection and we now believe that the altars were erected in a sacred area. As a result, no parade ground can be identified at Maryport.

There are references to Roman armies becoming slack through inactivity. Generals such as Scipio Aemilianus in Spain and Domitius Corbulo on the eastern frontier had to put their soldiers through rigorous training regimes before they were ready for fighting. This was a problem common to all armies. It is interesting that it happened in the Roman army because it would appear that provincial governors should have undertaken tours of inspection. In the time of Hadrian, Arrian was his governor of Cappadocia on the eastern frontier and he wrote an account of his inspection of the forts along the coast of the Black Sea, the only one which has survived from antiquity. Arrian implies that this was not the only occasion that he had inspected these military installations, but that he had been before with Hadrian himseslf. So, it is likely that successive governors of Britain came north from the provincial capital in London to inspect their regiments based at Maryport, and ensure that they were ready for combat.

Final thoughts

There is no doubt that further excavation would yield important results   Eric Birley

Maryport is a fascinating – and frustrating – site. The collection of Roman inscriptions and sculpture is the oldest in Britain still in private hands. It has descended through generations of the Eaglesfields, Senhouses, Pocklington Senhouses and Scott Plummers to the present day. It is indeed a collection to be proud of. Yet, we know frustratingly little of the find spots of many of the objects in the collection. Assumptions have been made, and modern excavations have proved them wrong. But, modern archaeologists have taken hold of the uncertainties, the ambiguities and frustrations and are teasing out new answers.

One way has been through geophysical survey. The fort and extra-mural settlement remain one of the most intensively and extensively examined sites of Roman Britain, but one which presents us with a challenge: how do we move on to explore the site? The complete excavation of the whole of the extra-mural settlement would be ruinously expensive (Figure 115). But if we only excavate a small area, or sample different areas, how sure can we be that these are representative of the whole settlement? The excavation of sample areas, however, does offer a chance to test the results produced by geophysics. We gained a significant insight through the excavation of the hill top where the altars were found in 1870 and its southern slopes; some of the evidence from the excavation did not match with what we think we can see from the geophysics.

Excavations always throw up challenges. We may be able to answer one question, but we create several others (Figure 116). Or, to put it another way, when one door closes, another opens. The discovery that the altars had not

FINAL THOUGHTS

Figure 115. The excavation of a house in the extra-mural settlement by Oxford Archaeology North in progress

Figure 116. A new altar, dedicated by T. Attius Tutor, found by Ian Haynes and Tony Wilmott, used as packing in the holes dug to receive the timbers of a building

been ritually buried, as believed for over 70 years, but had been used as supports for a timber structure, led not only to the demolition of one theory, but the stating of two new questions: what was the nature of the timber structure and where had the altars been originally placed? The answer to the former is difficult to resolve; at least a reasoned guess can be offered to the latter. Yet, there is a subsidiary question. The timber installation stood on the highest point of the hill; why had the Romans not used this for a building, perhaps the temple to Jupiter which one might have expected to have sat on such a point – after all the dedication was to Jupiter Capitolinus and his temple in Rome sat on a hill, the Capitoline Hill.

The excavation of the house in the extra-mural settlement by Oxford Archaeology North produced similar evidence for the shape and style of the building to that recorded by Joseph Robinson – though excavated to a far higher level of competence and with more detailed

Figure 117. Traditional images of the interior of Roman forts are, not surprisingly, dominated by males, but there is increasing evidence of the presence there of at least some women.
Drawn by Michael J. Moore

results. Interestingly, it provided information on one important aspect of the occupation of this part of the site, lacking in the past because of the paucity of the collection of archaeological artefacts, namely that the area had been abandoned in the late 3rd century, perhaps sometime during the two decades before 300. In that respect, the settlement falls into a pattern recognised elsewhere along Hadrian's Wall. But where did the inhabitants go? Some may have moved into the fort, but this does not seem large enough to have held all the civilians (Figure 117). Perhaps, however, the regiment was below strength, perhaps even well below owing to the turmoil of civil war and invasion throughout the empire at this time; possibly some of the unit had been withdrawn for service elsewhere. Either scenario would have had an effect on the rest of the military community at Maryport. These questions can only be answered by further excavation, both in the fort and in the civil settlement.

Another question for us is, when and how did the occupation of the fort end? The last coin found at the site dates to about 400 and there is pottery of about the same date. Other artefacts of that time are sparse, though the belt stiffeners may date to the late 4th century and indicate the presence of Roman soldiers

(Figure 118). The tombstones of Rianorix and [S]purcio also appear to date to the last years of occupation at the site (Figures 92 and 114). Here, may also lie the enigmatic timber building found on the summit of the hill. There is no evidence that the fort was destroyed by enemy action. It may be that military occupation of the site withered as the pay chests stopped arriving.

Figure 118. Two belt stiffeners, each about 38mm long, dating to the 4th century and indicating continuing occupation of the fort by the army at this time

This account of Maryport is an interim statement because the four excavations undertaken in recent years have not yet been published. In time, these reports will appear and then new information will be brought into the public domain. In the meantime, I hope that I have managed to convey something of the life of soldiers and civilians at Maryport 1800 years ago. It was a bustling, thriving community, visibly connected through its officers and supplies to provinces in modern Europe, North Africa and the Middle East. The evidence that it offers us for the careers of these officers remains of international importance.

The process also works in reverse for while the evidence from Maryport can cast light on the operation of the Roman army information from other parts of the Roman Empire may, in time, help us to understand the material found at Maryport better. One such possibility is the altar to the goddess Setlocenia (Figure 119). The name is Celtic and the dedicator was Labareus Ge[, which probably is an abbreviation for 'a German', but the goddess is otherwise unknown. If we are to learn more about the goddess, it will probably be as a result of a chance discovery in Germany. In the meantime, all we have is one altar dedicated to a deity whose name is believed to mean 'long life', an appropriate goddess for a soldier who wanted to survive the next battle to strike a bargain with.

Finally, to return to the collection. It is difficult to believe that the last word has been said about all these wonderful sculptured stones and inscriptions. They offer archaeological researchers a rich source of future investigations into the Roman army and into the religion of its soldiers and the fellow members of its community. Here indeed is a rich blessing bestowed on us by generations of Senhouses.

Figure 119. An altar to the goddess Setlocenia dedicated by Labareus, a German (RIB 841), reproduced as a woodcut in J. C. Bruce, *Lapidarium Septentrionale*, 875.

Acknowledgements

I am grateful to my fellow trustees and officials at Maryport for their support in preparing this book, and in particular Ian Carradice, Ian Caruana, Ian Francis and Bill Griffiths who read and commented on the text to its advantage. I thank Jane Laskey, Ian Caruana, Mel Johnson of CFA Archaeology Ltd, Stephen Rowland and John Zant of Oxford Archaeology North and Tony Wilmott for assistance with the collection of photographs. I am also grateful to Robert Bewley for discussion on Ewanrigg, Ian Haynes for reading the text and his helpful comments on the Roman army, Paul Holder for discussion about the regiments based at Maryport, Peter Hill for discussion of the altars, Natalie Mullen for comment on the Senhouse family, Ursula Rothe for information on the clothing of the women depicted on tombstones, David Taylor for comment on the buildings revealed by geophysical survey, and Angus Winchester for advice on place-names. Acknowledgement is provided in the captions for those colleagues and institutions who have kindly provided illustrations.

Further reading

The essential two publications about Roman Maryport are those edited by Roger Wilson and by Roger Wilson and Ian Caruana below. These contain a range of papers about the Netherhall collection and the fort and its setting. The first includes papers by Roger Wilson on current problems, Ian Caruana on the early years, Amy Lax and Keith Blood on the earthworks, David Breeze, John Mann and Peter Hill on the altars, Lindsay Allason-Jones on women, Jon Coulston on the sculpture and David Shotter on the coins. The papers directly relevant to Maryport in the second volume are Paul Holder on place-names, Keith Blood and Trevor Pearson on the survey of the site by RCHME, Alan Biggins and David Taylor on the geophysical survey, and Stephen Harbottle on Joseph Robinson.

Interim reports on the modern excavations appear in the journal *Britannia* 43 (2012) 294-5; 44 (2013) 190-1; 45 (2014) 325-8; 46 (2015) 296; 47 (2016) 303-4. Two longer articles were published in *Current Archaeology* 259 (2011) and 289 (2014).

Roman Maryport

Allason-Jones, L. 1997. The women of Roman Maryport. In R. J. A. Wilson (ed.): 92-111.

Ashmore, B. 1997. Senhouse of Netherhall – 1726 Achievement of Arms: recovery of an eighteenth-century masterpiece. In R. J. A. Wilson (ed.): 141-7.

Bailey, J. B. 1880. The Maryport camp: its history, its explorations and its present aspect. *Cumberland and Westmorland Association Transactions* 5: 181-90.

Bailey, J. B. 1915. Catalogue of Roman Inscribed and Sculptured Stones, Coins, Earthenware, etc., discovered in and near the Roman Fort at Maryport, and preserved at Netherhall. *Transactions of the Cumberland and Westmorland Antiquarian and Archaeological Society* 2 series, 15: 135-72.

Bailey, J. B. 1922. Recent finds at Maryport, *Transactions of the Cumberland and Westmorland Antiquarian and Archaeological Society* 2 series, 22: 462-3.

Bailey, J. B. 1923. 'Maryport and the Tenth Iter, with further notes on Roman antiquities', *Transactions of the Cumberland and Westmorland Antiquarian and Archaeological Society* 2 series, 23: 142-53.

Bailey, J. B. 1926. Further notes on Roman roads at Maryport and on the Netherhall Collection. *Transactions of the Cumberland and Westmorland Antiquarian and Archaeological Society* 2 series, 26: 414-22.

Bellhouse, R. L. nd [1992]. *Joseph Robinson of Maryport. Archaeologist extraordinary.* Otley: Smith Settle.

Biggins, J. A. and D. J. A. Taylor 2004. The Roman fort and *vicus* at Maryport: geophysical survey, 2000-2004. In R. J. A. Wilson and I. D. Caruana (eds): 102-33.

Birley, E. 1961. *Research on Hadrian's Wall*: 216-23. Kendal: Titus Wilson.

Breeze, D. J. 1997. The regiments stationed at Maryport and their commanders. In R. J. A. Wilson (ed.): 67-89.

Breeze, D. J., B. Dobson and V. A. Maxfield 2012. Maenius Agrippa, A Chronological Conundrum. *Acta Classica* 55: 17-30.

Bruce, J. C. 1870. Altars recently found in the Roman camp at Maryport. *Transactions of the Cumberland and Westmorland Antiquarian and Archaeological Society* 1 series, 1: 175-88.

Bruce, J. C. 1875. *Lapidarium Septentrionale*. London: Bernard Quaritch.

Camden, W. 1600. *Britannia*: 694-7. London: G. Bishop.

Collingwood, R. G. 1936. The Roman fort and settlement Maryport, *Transactions of the Cumberland and Westmorland Antiquarian and Archaeological Society* 2 series, 36: 85-99.

Coulston, J. C. N. 1997. The stone sculptures. In R. J. A. Wilson (ed.): 112-31.

Coulston, J. C. N. 2014. The Maryport altars revisited. In A. Busch and A. Schäfer (eds), *Römische Weihealtäre im Kontext*. Frieberg: Likias: 381-96.

Cummins, J. I. 1891. A Roman recreation ground: The Campus Martius of Glanoventa. *Transactions of the Cumberland and Westmorland Association for the Advancement of Literature and Science* 16: 13-21.

Edwards, B. J. N. 1998. *William Camden, his* Britannia *and some Roman Inscriptions*. Kendal: Titus Wilson.

Ferguson, R. S. 1880. Excavations at the Roman camp near Maryport, now believed to be the Axelodunum of the Notitia. *Proceedings of the Society of Antiquaries of London* 2 series, 58: 392-6.

Flynn, P. A. 2006a. Report of an archaeological evaluation at Sca Brows, Maryport, Cumbria. Unpublished interim report.

Flynn, P. A. 2006b. Interim report of an archaeological excavation at Sea Brows, Maryport, Cumbria. Unpublished interim report.

Gordon, A. 1726. *Itinerarium Septentrionale*: 98-100. London: G. Strahan.

Graafstal, E. P. 2012. Hadrian's haste: a priority programme for the Wall. *Archaeologia Aeliana* 5 series, 41: 123-84.

Harbottle, S. 2004. Joseph Robinson – a biographical note. In R. J. A. Wilson and I. D. Caruana (eds): 205-23.

Haverfield, F. 1916. The Netherhall Collection', *Transactions of the Cumberland and Westmorland Antiquarian and Archaeological Society* 2 series, 16: 284-6.

Haynes, I. and T. Wilmott 2011. Jupiter Best and Greatest. *Current Archaeology* 259: 20–25.

Haynes, I. and T. Wilmott 2014. Maryport's Mystery Monuments. *Current Archaeology* 289: 17–21.

Head, E. 1773. An account of some antiquities discovered, on digging into a large Roman barrow, at Ellenborough, in Cumberland, 1763 [1742]. *Archaeologia* 2: 54-9.

Hepple, L. W. 2001 '"The museum in the garden": displaying classical antiquities in Elizabethan and Jacobean England. *Garden History*, 29, 2: 109-20.

Hill, P. R. 1997. The Maryport altars: some first thoughts. In R. J. A. Wilson (ed.): 92-104.

Holder, P. 2004. Roman place-names on the Cumbrian coast. In R. J. A. Wilson and I. D. Caruana (eds): 52-65.

Horsley, J. 1732. *Britannia Romana*. London: John Osborn and Thomas Longman.

Jarrett, M. G. 1954. A Christian monogram from Roman Maryport. *Transactions of the Cumberland and Westmorland Antiquarian and Archaeological Society* 2 series, 54: 268-71.

Jarrett, M. G. 1958. The pre-Hadrianic occupation of Roman Maryport. *Transactions of the Cumberland and Westmorland Antiquarian and Archaeological Society* 2 series, 58: 63-7.

Jarrett, M. G. 1965. Roman officers at Maryport. *Transactions of the Cumberland and Westmorland Antiquarian and Archaeological Society* 2 series, 65: 115-32.

Jarrett, M. G. 1976. *Maryport, Cumbria: A Roman Fort and its Garrison*. Kendal: Titus Wilson.

Lax, A. and Blood, K. 1997. The earthworks of the Maryport fort: an analytical field survey by the Royal Commission on the Historical Monuments of England. In R. J. A. Wilson (ed.): 52-66.

Mann, J. C. 1997. A note on the Maryport altars. In R. J. A. Wilson (ed.): 90-1.

Pennant, T. 1776. *A Tour in Scotland, and Voyage to the Hebrides, 1772*: 59-64. London: Benjamin White.

Robinson, J. 1881. Notes on the excavations near the Roman camp, Maryport, during the year 1880. *Transactions of the Cumberland and Westmorland Antiquarian and Archaeological Society* 1 series, 5: 237-57.

Rooke, H. 1792 An account of some Roman antiquities in Cumberland hitherto unnoticed. *Archaeologia* 10: 137-42.

Shotter, D. 1997. Roman coins from Maryport. In R. J. A. Wilson (ed.): 132-40.

Stukeley, W. 1776. *Itinerarium Curiosum*: 49-51. London: Baker and Leigh.

Waldock, S. 2002. Maryport Parade-grounds. In P. R. Hill (ed.), *Polybius to Vegetius*: 109-23. The Hadrianic Society.

Webster, J. 1986. Roman bronzes from Maryport in the Netherhall Collection. *Transactions of the Cumberland and Westmorland Antiquarian and Archaeological Society* 2 series, 86: 47-70.

Wenham, L. P. 1939. Notes on the garrisoning of Maryport. *Transactions of the Cumberland and Westmorland Antiquarian and Archaeological Society* 2 series, 39: 19-30.

Wilson, R. J. A. (ed.) 1997. *Roman Maryport and its Setting. Essays in Memory of Michael G. Jarrett*. Kendal: Trustees of Senhouse Roman Museum.

Wilson, R. J. A. and I. D. Caruana (eds) 2004. *Romans on the Solway. Essays in Honour of Richard Bellhouse*. Kendal: Trustees of Senhouse Roman Museum.

The Senhouse family

Hughes, E. 1965. *North Country Life in the Eighteenth Century. Volume 2, Cumberland and Westmorland, 1700-1830*. Oxford: Oxford University Press.

Mullen, N. 2015. The Last Century of the Senhouses: Gentry Paternalism in Maryport, 1848-1952. Unpublished MA Dissertation, Lancaster University.

Senhouse, R. M. le F. (Miss) 1893. Senhouse of Seascale Hall, in Cumberland. *Transactions of the Cumberland and Westmorland Antiquarian and Archaeological Society* 1 series, 12: 247-60.

Maryport

Cumbria County History Trust, on-line entries on Maryport, Cross Canonby, and Ellenborough and Ewanrigg.

Hadrian's Wall

Breeze, D. J. 2006. *J. Collingwood Bruce's Handbook to the Roman Wall*. Newcastle: Society of Antiquaries of Newcastle upon Tyne.

Breeze, D. J. and B. Dobson 2000. *Hadrian's Wall*. 4th edition. London: Penguin.

Hodgson, N. 2017. *Hadrian's Wall. Archaeology and History at the limit of Rome's Empire*. Marlborough: Robert Hale.

Hingley, R. C. 2012. *Hadrian's Wall. A Life*. Oxford: Oxford University Press.

The Roman army and Roman administration

Birley, A. R. 2003. *The Government of Britain*. Oxford: Oxford University Press.

Breeze, D. J. 2016. *The Roman Army*. London: Bloomsbury.

Davies, R. W. 1989. *Service in the Roman Army*. Edinburgh: Edinburgh University Press.

Goldsworthy, A. 2003. *The Complete Roman Army*. London: Thames and Hudson.

Haynes, I. 2013. *The Blood of the Provinces*. Oxford: Oxford University Press.

Holder, P. A. 1982. *The Roman Army in Britain*. London: Batsford.

Keppie, L. J. F. 1998. *The Making of the Roman Army*. London: Batsford.

MacMullen, R. 1963. *Soldier and Civilian in the Later Roman Empire*. Cambridge (MA): Harvard University Press.

Phang, S. E. 2008. *Roman Military Service. Ideologies of Discipline in the Late Republic and Early Principate*. New York: Cambridge University Press.

Rivet, A. L. F. and Smith, C. 1979. *The Place-Names of Roman Britain*. London: Batsford.

Roman forts

Bidwell, P. 2007. *Roman Forts in Britain*. Stroud: Tempus.

Breeze, D. J. 2002. *Roman Forts in Britain*. Botley: Shire.

Roman frontiers

Austen, N. J. E. and N. B. Rankov 1995. *Exploratio: Military and Political Intelligence in the Roman World from the Second Punic War to the Battle of Adrianople*. London: Routledge.

Breeze, D. J. 2013. *The Frontiers of Imperial Rome*. Barnsley: Pen and Sword.

Mattern, S. P. 1999. *Rome and the Enemy*. Berkeley and Los Angeles: University of California Press.

Whittaker, C. R. 1994. *Frontiers of the Roman Empire. A Social and Economic Study*. Baltimore and London: John Hopkins University.

Roman Women

Allason-Jones, L. 2005. *Women in Roman Britain*. York: Council for British Archaeology.

Croom, A. 2011. *Running the Roman Home*. Stroud: History Press.

Roman religion

Green, M. A. 1986. *The Gods of the Celts*. Gloucester: Alan Sutton.

Ross, A. 1967. *Pagan Celtic Britain. Studies in Iconography and Tradition*. London: Routledge Kegan & Paul.

Rural settlements

Bewley, R. H. 1992. Excavation on Two Crop-Mark Sites in the Solway Plain, Cumbria. Ewanrigg Settlement and Swarthy Hill 1986-1988. *Transactions of the Cumberland and Westmorland Antiquarian and Archaeological Society* 2 series, 92: 23-47.

Bewley, R. H., I. H. Longworth, S. Browne and J. P. Huntley 1992. Excavations of a Bronze Age cremation cemetery at Ewanrigg, Maryport, Cumbria. *Proceedings of the Prehistoric Society* 58: 325-354.

Bewley, R. H. 1994. *Prehistoric and Romano-British Settlement in the Solway Plan, Cumbria* (Oxbow Monograph 36). Oxford: Oxbow.

Higham, N. J. and G. D. B. Jones 1975. Frontiers, forts and farmers: Cumbrian aerial survey 1974-5, *Archaeological Journal* 132: 16-53.

Ancient Sources

The following provide direct information on life in the Roman army through surviving ancient documents.

Bowman, A. K. and J. D. Thomas 1994. *The Vindolanda Writing Tablets II*. London: The British Museum.

Bowman, A. K. and J. D. Thomas 2003. *The Vindolanda Writing Tablets III*. London: The British Museum.

Campbell, B. 1994. *The Roman Army 31 BC – AD 337: A Source Book*. London: Routledge.

Tomlin, R. S. O. 1998. Roman manuscripts from Carlisle: the ink-written tablets. *Britannia* 29: 31-84.

The inscriptions found at Maryport are published in the volumes known together as *The Roman Inscriptions of Britain*.
The Letters of the Younger Pliny, published by Penguin, are available in translation.

Index

Note: Maryport, museum and sculpture are not indexed

Aelius Sacas[, 40
Africa, 31, 32, 35, 38, 69, 101, 105
Alauna, 18, 20
Allason-Jones, Lindsay, archaeologist, 44, 108
Alneburgh Hall, 3, 4
altars, 1–2, 4–5, 7–11, 13, 15–16, 28–29, 31–32, 39, 44, 55–56, 58–61, 63, 65, 75–76, 101–103, 107–108
Antistius Verianus, L., prefect, 31, 38, 59-60
Antonine Wall, 26-7, 34, 54, 59, 65, 95, 97
Antoninus Pius, emperor, 33–34, 53, 95–96
Ardoch, fort, 29
Arrian, Roman military author, 101
Asclepius, god, 41–42
Ashmore, Lt. Col. Brian, saviour of the Netherhall collection, 2, 12, 15
Attacotti, Irish tribe, 21, 98
Attius Tutor, T., prefect, 34–35, 66, 70, 76, 103
Bailey, J. B., author, 1, 11
bangle, glass, 46-47
Bar Kokhba uprising, 35, 95
barrack-blocks, 23–25
bastions at fort, 21, 99
bath-house, 8, 23
Battery, the Naval Reserve Training Battery, 2, 12, 14–15

Belatucadrus, god, 8, 54, 72
Bewley, Dr Robert, archaeologist, 87–88, 90, 107
Biggins, J. Alan, geophysisist, 24, 48–50, 108
Birdoswald, fort, 22, 61, 85
Birley, Professor Tony, ancient historian, 11
Birrens, fort, 85, 92
bones, 10, 53, 77–78, 87
Bowness-on-Solway, fort, 9, 19, 85, 86, 97
Bridgeness distance slab, 59
Brigantes, tribe, 73
British Museum, 6, 8
Bruce, J Collingwood, author, 6–7, 8, 9, 22, 28, 45, 47, 50, 56, 65, 71, 106
burials, 11, 16, 77–78, 87
Caballius Priscus, C., tribune, 31–32, 55, 57, 59–60, 75
Caecilius Vegetus, prefect, 33
Caledonians, 95–97
Camden, William, antiquarian and author, 1, 5, 7–8, 11, 17, 70
Cammius Maximus, L., prefect, 29, 31, 35, 38, 60
camp, 26-7
camp followers, 43
Capitoline Hill, Rome, 103
Cardiff, fort, 98

Carlisle, 54, 76, 78, 85, 86, 91
Carvetii, tribe, 54, 72
Carvoran, fort, 54, 85
Castle Hill, Maryport, 3, 11
cavalry, 12, 24, 29-30, 35, 82, 101
Celtic gods, 74, 81
cemeteries, 16, 77-81, 87
Censorius Cornelianus, M., prefect,16, 31, 35, 39, 59-60
centurion, 24, 35, 39-40, 44
ceremonies, religious, 58, 65, 76, 81
CFA Archaeology Ltd, 2, 16, 78, 87-89, 107
Chesters, fort, 22-23, 33, 85
Child, F. A., draughtsman, 22, 46, 77-78
child, tombstone of, 22, 46, 77-78
Christianity, 12, 76, 78
circular building, 16, 50, 51, 62, 65, 77, 80
citizenship, Roman, 29, 34, 43-45, 96
clothing, 45-47, 83
coastal defense, 21, 97-99
cohorts, 17-18, 28-35
   Eighteenth Cohort of Volunteers, 35, 38
   First Cohort of Baetasians, 17-8, 34-35, 66, 69, 70, 96
   First Cohort of Dalmatians, 17, 33-34
   First Cohort of Spaniards, 8, 17, 25, 29-32, 35, 39, 42, 55, 58, 67, 70, 75, 96, 100
   Third Cohort of Nervians, 20
coins, 10-11, 25, 28, 50, 104, 108
cone, fir, 77
Connelly, Peter, artist and historian, 30
Cornelius Peregrinus, C., tribune, 6, 31-33, 58, 69
Cotton, Sir Robert, antiquarian, 1, 5-8
Coulston, Jon, archaeologist, 66-67, 70, 82, 108
Criffel, hill, 18-19, 94-95, 103
Crosscannoby, 3, 8, 11
Cumberland and Westmorland Antiquarian and Archaeological Society, 11, 90
Cumbrian coast, 17, 25, 97
Cummins, Father J. I., 10-11, 101
Curzon family, 3
Dacia, province, 35, 94

Danube, river, 17, 35, 93
deployment, military, 25, 85, 97
diplomas, 29, 33, 34
ditches, 7, 21, 48, 50, 65, 85-88, 100
D]occei on amphora, 40
doctors in the Roman army, 41-2
dress, 45-46
Eaglesfield family, 3, 4-5, 7, 102
Egnatius Pastor, A., 41-42, 44
Ellen, river, 3, 11, 14, 17, 20, 49, 78, 84
Ellenburgh, 1, 3
Ellenfoot, 3
end of Roman Maryport, 28, 65, 99, 104-105
Epona, goddess, 75
Ewanrigg, settlement, 87-88, 90, 107
excavations, 1, 2, 11-12, 16, 24, 102
extra-mural settlement, 1-2, 16, 40, 48-54, 63, 77, 87, 88, 91, 102-104
families of soldiers, 43
Farington, Joseph, artist, 19
farms, 16, 86-91
Flynn, Paul, archaeologist, 26
food, 78, 86, 87, 88
fort, vi, 1-4, 7, 9-12, 16, 17-30, 33-35, 39, 43-44, 48, 50, 52, 54-55, 58, 61, 66, 69, 75, 77-78, 80, 84-88, 90-92, 94, 96-102, 104-105, 108
Fortuna, goddess, 69, 72
Galatia, province, 40-41
gates, 8, 9, 11, 21-23
Genius, god, 8, 72-73
geophysical survey, 16, 23-25, 48-50, 87, 102, 107-108
Germany/Germans, 18, 33, 41-42, 60, 72, 105
Gordian III, emperor, 28
Gordon, Alexander, antiquarian, 7, 8
granaries, 23, 50, 100
Green, Miranda, author, 75
Hadrian, emperor, 9, 20, 22-23, 25-26, 29, 31-33, 38, 44, 48, 54, 58, 69, 86, 94-95, 97-98, 100-101, 104
Hadrian's Wall, 9, 20, 22-23, 25, 29, 33, 48, 54, 69, 85, 86, 94-95, 97-98, 100, 104

Haynes, Professor Ian, archaeologist, 2, 16, 26–27, 56, 60, 63–65, 78–79, 85, 103, 107
Head, Rev Erasmus, 3, 10, 66, 69–70, 72, 80–81, 83
headquarters building, 7–8, 9, 23
Helstrius Novellus, prefect, 31–32, 59–61, 67, 75
Hercules, god, 67–68
Hermione, 40, 44, 70–71
Hill, Peter, stone mason, 60-61, 76
Honorius, emperor, 10, 25, 96
horned gods, 73-4
Housesteads, fort, 20, 22, 54, 56, 85
Indutius, tile maker, 41–42
inscriptions, 1, 7, 11–12, 25, 27–35, 38–42, 55, 72, 101–102, 105, 113
Irish Sea, 17, 98
Italy, 30–31, 35
Jarrett, Professor Michael, archaeologist and chair of the Senhouse Museum Trust, 11–12, 15, 61, 76
Jones, Barri, archaeologist, 86, 91
Judaea, province, 35, 39, 95
Julia Martina, 44–45
Julius Caesar, general, 43, 93
Julius Civilis, *optio*, 40, 72
Julius Marinus, centurion, 39–40, 44
Julius Senecianus, 40, 77
Julius Simplex, 40, 44
Juno, goddess, 44, 76
Jupiter, god, 8–9, 29, 31–32, 38–39, 55, 58–61, 65–66, 76, 101, 103
Karus, 40
King's Burying Place, 10 see also Pudding Pie Hill
Labareus, 18, 40, 72, 105–106
Lancaster, fort, 21, 81, 85, 98
legions, 27
  Second Legion, 27
  Ten Fretensis, 35
  Twentieth Legion, 27–28
location of fort, 17, 18, 19, 63, 84–85
Luca, 44
Maenius Agrippa, M., tribune, 30–31, 35, 38, 55, 59–60, 75

Mann, John, ancient historian, 20, 108
Marcus Septimius, 40, 74
Maritima, 39, 44
marriage, 3, 43
Mars, god, 66–67, 76
Maryport and District Archaeological Society, 2, 16, 101
Mercury, god, 67, 69
milefortlets, 87, 97
military deployment, 25, 85, 97
Minerva, goddess, 67–68, 76
Moore, Michael J., artist, 93, 104
Moriregis, 40
Moresby, fort, 25, 85, 86
name of Maryport fort, 18-19
naval duties, 100
Nemausus, city, 35, 39
Neptune, god, 66–67
Netherhall, 1–4, 7–8, 10, 12–14, 50, 70, 108
Newcastle, 2, 7, 9, 16, 56, 95
Noricum, province, 34–35
north gate, 8–9, 11, 21, 48
Notitia Dignitatum, Roman document, 18, 20, 29
Nymphs, 71–72
Osterburken, fort, 60–61
Oxford Archaeology, 2, 16, 53–54, 103, 107
Papcastle, fort, 78, 85, 86, 91
parade ground, 10–11, 100-101
Pennant, Thomas, antiquarian, 7–8, 10
phallic symbols, 73-4, 80-1
Picts, 96, 97
pits, 10, 55–56, 78, 85, 87
Pliny, Roman writer and governor, 38, 55, 57–58, 60
Postumius Acilianus, prefect, 33–34
pottery, 11, 28, 40, 50, 52–53, 65, 78, 85, 87, 104
prefects, 29–34
Pudding Pie Hill, 8, 10–11, 26, 101
quarries, 15
Quintus, 40, 44
radiocarbon dates, 87, 88
ramparts, 7, 20
Ravenna Cosmography, Roman document, 18

Ravenglass, fort, 19
religion, Roman, 58-76, 105
Rianorix, 78–79, 99, 105
roads, 11, 22–23, 25, 48, 49, 50, 51, 77–78, 80, 85-87, 91
Robinson, Joseph, archaeologist, 1, 8, 11, 40, 50–52, 61–63, 77, 103, 108
Rome, 9, 19, 30, 59, 66, 69, 76, 95–96, 103
rural settlements, 16, 48, 86-91
Saldae, Roman city, 32
Scipio Aemilianus, general, 43, 101
Scots, 21, 96, 98
Scott Plummer, Joe, 1–2
Senhouse family, 1, 3, 4, 8, 15, 60, 102, 107
  Elizabeth, 1, 4
  Guy, 9, 12
  Humphrey I, 1, 8, 9
  Humphrey II, 10
  Humprey III, 8
  John, 1, 4–5, 7-9, 20
  Mary, 1, 3
  Roger, 12, 100, 108
Senhouse Museum Trust, 1–2, 15–16, 48, 49
Septimius Severus, emperor, 94, 96
Serpent stone, 11, 50, 73, 77, 80–81
Setlocenia, goddess, 72, 75, 105-6
Sirmium, Roman fort, 60-1
Skinburness, 9
slaves, 43–44, 46
Sol, god, 72–73
Solva, Roman city, 34–35
Solway estuary, 17–18, 21-22, 49, 94, 100
Sotera, 44, 77
Spain, 34–35, 43, 101
[S]purcio, 99, 105
standard bearer, 40
stone masons, 76
stone robbing, 12
strength of army units, 29-31, 92
strong room, 7–8, 100
Stukeley, William, antiquarian, 5, 7, 12, 17, 43
supplies, 60, 88, 91, 96, 100
Swarthy Hill, 87, 90, 97

Taylor, D. J. A., architect and historian, 24, 48–50, 107–108
temple, 11, 16, 27, 50, 51, 60–65, 66, 103
tiles, 41-42, 50
Tirunc(ulus), 40
tombstones, 40, 45–46, 77–79, 82–83, 99, 105, 107
training, 100-101
Trajan, emperor, 34, 55, 57–58, 60, 94
tribunes, 31–32, 100
Ulpius Titianus, prefect, 34, 76
Valour of the Emperor, 44, 70–71
Vegetius, Roman military author, 100
Venus, goddess, 67–68
Victory, goddess, 56, 65, 69–70, 95
Vindolanda, 54, 60, 69, 85, 95
Vireius Paul[, 40
Vulcan, god, 66–67
Waldock, Shirley, 10
warfare in Britain, 95-9
Wilmott, Tony, archaeologist, 2, 16, 26–27, 56, 60, 63–65, 78–79, 85, 103, 107
women, 43–47, 104, 107–108
York, legionary fortress, 20, 85, 96

Also by David Breeze:

Bearsden. The Story of a Roman Fort
Archaeopress 2016. ISBN 978 178491 490 5

The Roman fort at Bearsden and its annexe, together with areas beyond its defences, were extensively excavated from 1973 to 1982. The report on these excavations was published in 2016. This 'popular' account of the discoveries looks at the material recovered from the site in a different way, examining the process of archaeological excavation, the life of the soldiers at the fort based on the results of the excavation as well as material from elsewhere in the Roman Empire, the presentation and interpretation of the bath-house and latrine, and a discussion of possible future work arising out of the excavation. The excavation report was well illustrated with reconstruction drawings and the process of creating these is also discussed.

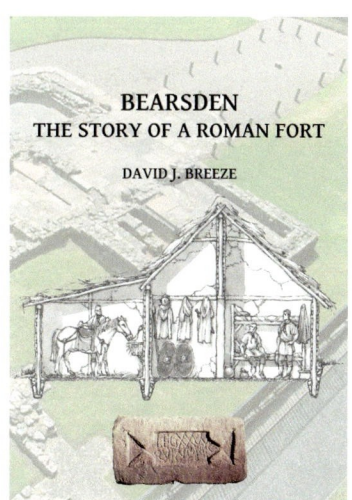

For a wider perspective on Roman frontiers:

Proceedings of the XXI International Congress of Roman Frontier Studies (Limes Congress) held at Newcastle upon Tyne in August 2009 edited by Nick Hodgson, Paul Bidwell and Judith Schachtmann. Archaeopress Roman Archaeology 25. 2017. ISBN 978 178491 590 2

Sixty years after the first Congress, delegates could reflect on how the Congress has grown and changed over six decades and could be heartened at the presence of so many young scholars and a variety of topics and avenues of research into the army and frontiers of the Roman empire that would not have been considered in 1949.

Papers are organised into the same thematic sessions as in the actual conference: Women and Families in the Roman Army; Roman Roads; The Roman Frontier in Wales; The Eastern and North African Frontiers; Smaller Structures: towers and fortlets; Recognising Differences in Lifestyles through Material Culture; Barbaricum; Britain; Roman Frontiers in a Globalised World; Civil Settlements; Death and Commemoration; Danubian and Balkan Provinces; Camps; Logistics and Supply; The Germanies and Augustan and Tiberian Germany; Spain; Frontier Fleets.

This wide-ranging collection of papers enriches the study of Roman frontiers in all their aspects.